RESPONSE ABLE

MATTHEW HAGEE

CHARISMA
HOUSE

Most CHARISMA HOUSE BOOK GROUP products are available at special quantity discounts for bulk purchase for sales promotions, premiums, fund-raising, and educational needs. For details, write Charisma House Book Group, 600 Rinehart Road, Lake Mary, Florida 32746, or telephone (407) 333-0600.

RESPONSE-ABLE by Matthew Hagee
Published by Charisma House
Charisma Media/Charisma House Book Group
600 Rinehart Road
Lake Mary, Florida 32746
www.charismahouse.com

Unless otherwise noted, all Scripture quotations are from the New King James Version of the Bible. Copyright © 1979, 1980, 1982 by Thomas Nelson, Inc., publishers. Used by permission.

Scripture quotations marked KJV are from the King James Version of the Bible.

Scripture quotations marked NIV are from the Holy Bible, New International Version. Copyright © 1973, 1978, 1984, International Bible Society. Used by permission.

Cover design by Justin Evans
Design Director: Bill Johnson

Visit the author's website at www.jhm.org.

Library of Congress Cataloging-in-Publication Data:
Hagee, Matthew.
  Response-able / Matthew Hagee.
     p. cm.
  Includes bibliographical references.
  ISBN 978-1-61638-136-3 (trade paper) -- ISBN 978-1-61638-419-7
(e-book) 1. Christian life. 2. Responsibility. I. Title.
  BV4501.3.H3454 2011
  248.4--dc22

                                2011007913

E-book ISBN: 978-1-61638-419-7

11 12 13 14 15 — 987654321
Printed in the United States of America

Contents

Section 1: You Are Always Able to Respond
Seven Lessons of Personal Responsibility

Section 2: Social Response-Ability
Seven Lessons That Will Change the World Around You

Section 3: Financial Response-Ability
Seven Lessons of Financial Responsibility

Section 4: The Educational Response-Ability
Seven Lessons That Will Change the Future of Education

Section 5: Political Response-Ability
Seven Lessons to Make a Political Difference

Foreword

MATTHEW HAS WRITTEN a fabulous book with the thought-provoking title of *Response-Able*. It means that you as an individual are always *able* to make an intelligent and godly *response* in every dimension of your life.

Winston Churchill said, "The price of greatness is responsibility."[1] It's not what happens to you that determines your destiny; it's how you respond to what happens to you that either makes or breaks you!

If you would learn self-mastery...if you would become fully and totally *response-able*, begin by yielding yourself to the one great Master.

Solomon expressed in this way: "He who is slow to anger is better than the mighty, and he who rules his spirit than he who takes a city" (Proverbs 16:32). The person who can control himself or herself in every environment is *response-able*.

Matthew covers the areas of personal, social, financial, educational, and political responsibility that will enrich and change your life forever! Enjoy this page-turner from the fresh breeze coming from the next generation.

—JOHN HAGEE

Introduction

I HAVE BEEN TOLD more than once in my life that I am an "old soul" in a young man's body, and as I observe the world around me, I believe those words are more accurate than I would like to admit.

I am my father's son, and have been without a doubt or apology since the day I was born. In 1978 fathers were not allowed in the delivery room. They were left to wait outside, nervously pacing until the nurse would bring word of the results of "It's a boy" or "It's a girl." On the occasion of my birth, my parents made it to the hospital with barely enough time to get out of their street clothes and into the pale green gowns before the nurse announced, "Doctor or no doctor, it's time to have a baby!" A few short minutes later, I arrived into the world with my father watching over the nurse's shoulder. The doctor burst through the door in just enough time to cut the umbilical cord. The first arms that I was placed in were my dad's, and we have remained that close ever since.

Throughout every chapter and page of my life, my father has been my teacher, leader, defender, and friend. He has always inspired me much more through his actions than he ever has by his words. To say it simply, he behaves like he believes, and in doing so has inspired me to believe as well. My desire is that once you have finished this book, you will be a believer too.

I want you to believe in your ability to make a change no matter what is stacked against you. I want you to believe that even though you may not be the cause of your circumstance, you have the power to affect it. I want you to believe that no matter who you are, where you come from, or what you are going through, you have the ability to respond to the world around you and make a huge impact on your quality of life in the future. That's the nature of the title of this work

Response-Able. Even though you may not be responsible for where you are, you are always able to respond.

Among the most valuable lessons that my father has taught me is to always consider what you can do rather than focus on what you can't. When you absorb all that is wrong in the world around you, it's easy to believe that the problems are so massive there is nothing you can do about it. That overwhelming sense of hopelessness can actually create a level of comfort, because after all, the world's problems are so big you can't be held responsible to fix them!

I've been taught otherwise. Each of us has a measure of responsibility on some level. Physically, financially, socially, emotionally, or spiritually, you must respond to happenings around you so that as they unfold, you are fulfilling your role as an agent for change and improvement. "It's not my fault" has never been a suitable excuse and only leads to dead-end roads, but when you turn the final page of this book, I believe you will see why you are the person who has been chosen for the challenge, and I know you will be compelled to respond.

If your life is on a course that you would indeed like to change, *you can change it.* How and when you turn things around is up to you, but it is a matter of your choice nonetheless. Your destiny is yours to determine unless you decide to forfeit the privilege. The circumstances of the moment may not be of your choosing, but how you respond to them is. So I think the only natural question to ask is this: *What are you going to do now?*

The question "What are we going to do?" is asked often but is seldom settled. It is used concerning all matters both great and small, and everyone wants to know, "What are we going to do?"

The daily questions:

- What are we going to do about dinner?

- What are we going to do on Friday night?

- What are we going to do after church Sunday?

The financial questions:

- What are we going to do about the mortgage?

- What are we going to do about retirement?

- What are we going to do about the children's college expenses?

- What are we going to do about the rising cost of health care?

The national and global questions:

- What are we going to do about government spending?

- What are we going to do about the worldwide threat of terror?

- What are we going to do about the global economy?

No matter how mundane the daily questions, or how deep and thought-provoking the financial, national, and global questions, these questions often seem more readily answered with the old tried and true: "I don't know. What do *you* want to do?" The point? Until *you* are willing to take a position of personal responsibility in your situation, you will not be able to determine or achieve the outcome that you're looking for. You will always have the terms dictated to you, and believe me, there are plenty of dictators in the world just looking for an opportunity to control your future. Whether they get their chance or not is truly up to you. As long as you are able to respond, the outcome is up to you.

There isn't an area of life that doesn't require a response. We are required to respond. We must respond politically. We cannot afford to continue abusing the future generations of this nation for what seems to be popular and convenient today. We must have the courage to abandon the mind-set of entitlement and embrace a lifestyle of political integrity.

With the proper response in government, we can then create needed change economically. From my earliest years my father made it very clear that you cannot spend what you do not possess. You may say, "Ah yes, but what about credit?" You do not spend on credit; you borrow against it, and what you are borrowing against is your future ability to pay for what you have claimed today. Currently we have borrowed against our future fortunes…against our children's and our children's children's futures to an amount that staggers the mind to calculate. You may feel as though it is your right when you turn eighteen to swipe a plastic card and dig yourself into a hole you will never get out of, but regardless of what you've seen others do, you are responsible for your own financial well-being and must be able to respond by taking the position *If I don't have it, I can't spend it.*

When you live an economically responsible life, you will find more resources are available to enable you to impact change and take responsibility in other areas also. The number one answer as to why people do not do more is because they do not have more to do it with.

What if the churches of America had enough resources to feed every hungry person in their cities? What if they had the resources to educate every child who desired to be taught in an environment where respect for God was encouraged rather than opposed, shunned, and oppressed? What if there were opportunities for churches to create jobs to empower people to help change the lives of others and to give everyone the opportunity to give back in the same way that they had received? Many of you might think that kind of world is beyond the realm of reality. In the pages of this book I want to show you that through personal responsibility and a proper response, you can revolutionize the world around you.

We must be response-able in the arena of education. One of the most powerful statements I have ever read concerning education came from a self-taught man who got his primary education in a log cabin in Illinois reading from the Bible. Abraham Lincoln said, *"The philosophy of the classroom today will be the philosophy of government tomorrow."* Without a doubt, the education system in this country has to turn around, and it's our responsibility to do it.

Did you know today's elementary school students are being introduced to Greek mythological deities, but the areas of reading, writing, and mathematics are being neglected? Colleges and universities are filled with international students who come from nations with barely 10 percent of the resources we have, and they have come to study how to shape the futures of their nations. Yet our homegrown students are failing the entrance exams. If we were to look closely at the impact the educational system in this country has had on America's future, we would have to consider it an act of war! Unless we respond, the futures of our children, their nation, and their world will be a change we answer for.

Hopefully in this book you will begin to see how all of these things are interconnected. They are like the waves created in a small pond when a large rock is thrown in. At first there seems to be a bit of a disturbance, and then the circles get larger and larger until the entire surface of the water is changed. So, where is the rock that needs to disturb these waters? Where is the agent of change who is waiting to be engaged? That's where you come in! If we are going to change our world, our nation, our politics, our economy, our society, our education, our current situation, and our quality of life tomorrow, *you* are going to have to get in the water. The time has come for this generation to take responsibility for tomorrow, and the response begins with you.

YOU ARE ALWAYS ABLE TO RESPOND

Seven Lessons of Personal Responsibility

AS I LEARN more about my life and observe how others live their lives, one thing has become crystal clear: You are always able to respond.

In 2006 my father led the effort to unite Christian leaders from around the country for the sake of the biblical mandate to support Israel. In February of that year, the first-ever meeting of Christians United for Israel (CUFI) took place. Later on that summer, in the month of July, the four hundred plus pastors and leaders who were in the February meeting brought more than three thousand people to Washington DC to meet with senators and congressmen to let them know personally that as voting Americans, we were very concerned about the welfare of the nation of Israel and that we fully expected them to be supportive of our ally in the Middle East.

The success of the event, by all observations, was overwhelming and indeed surpassed expectations, but for me, there was a moment in that first Christians United for Israel Summit that I will never forget. My father, along with select members of the executive board, was holding a press conference in the Hilton Hotel. Members of the media from all organizations, both friendly and hostile, were there with their questions, which ranged from suspicious and accusatory to investigative and journalistic. I simply took a seat in the back of the room to observe him, as a son who was watching his father do what he has always done, stand up and speak up for Israel.

It didn't take long for the question to be asked, "Pastor Hagee, why did you start this organization, and what are your long-term goals?" My father began the answer with a very familiar story to me about what had caused him to have the very first "Night to Honor Israel," which was held in in 1981 in San Antonio, Texas, following the world's outrage over Israel's strategic military strike on Saddam Hussein's nuclear reactor in Iraq. *Could you imagine anyone attacking Saddam Hussein for representing a threat to the security and well-being of the rest of the world?*

I was three years old when the first Night to Honor Israel took place, so hearing the retelling of the story was not an earthshaking revelation on that particular afternoon. My father has always, both publicly from the pulpit and privately in our own home, been passionate about supporting the "apple of God's eye." The sentence that took my breath away and left me to ponder for the next few days came at the conclusion of my father's answer to the obviously hostile reporter from Reuter News Service. After he had explained his more than twenty-five years of staunch support for Israel, he finished by saying these words: "And I feel that I was born for this moment right here and right now." Those are words I will never forget. In July of 2006 Dr. John Hagee was not short on accomplishment by anyone's standards, and yet in spite of all that he had already achieved, roles he had played, areas of service to the greater good provided, at the age of sixty-six I heard him say that he finally felt as though he had accomplished his purpose.

For me that was a very heavy statement. My dad doesn't throw around words for the purpose of poetic moments. If he says it, he means it. I have had a front-row seat and have seen firsthand in every arena all that his life's work has accomplished since 1978 to now. There was the birth of the television ministry, which reaches millions around the globe; the writing of more than twenty-five literary works, which have topped the best-sellers' lists on more than one occasion; the building of one of the finest churches in America, which is continuing to grow and thrive; and not to mention the raising of five children who are all married and living relatively successful lives. This short list is not all inclusive, but it simply provides a few of the things that in my mind would have given my then sixty-six-year-old father the privilege to say, "Look at all that I have achieved. I've earned the right to enjoy my work and take my rest. Thank you very much." However, the answer I heard him give to that small-minded journalist was loud and clear to me. That in my father's mind he had only just begun to really fulfill his purpose. Needless to say, I was blown away.

Later on that night in my hotel room, I replayed those words over and over again, and from them I extracted this lesson that I want to share with you now: *You are always able to respond.* First, consider that in 1981, as the world saw a bold military action taken against a major tyrant and as global leaders stood up in outrage, a relatively unknown pastor in South Texas stood up to applaud the only way he knew how. Some may have thought, "What good will he do? What difference will he make?" Yet, thirty years later, Christians United for Israel has more than six hundred thousand members and is growing stronger every day. In addition, consider his actions in 2006. At the age of sixty-six, when others might have said, "I've done all I can do; let someone else carry the ball," he stood up once again and took his support for Israel to an entirely new level. That night I learned that life accomplishments are never really complete.

No matter how renowned or unknown the person may be, there is a series of stages that have a commencement and a completion followed by yet another commencement as a new chapter of life begins.

To illustrate this point, consider the stage of life I am in right now. My wife, Kendal, and I have three beautiful children and are immersed in the process of raising a family. Hannah is five, John William is four, and Joel Charles celebrated his first birthday a few months ago. Every day spent with my young family is an adventure. It's not a matter of *if* our children will get into something—accurately stated it is, what *will* they get into *next*? I can see things that remind me of my childhood in each of my children, and, in my behavior as a young father, I often reflect on what my father instilled in me. You see, I have completed my stage as a child and have launched into my chapter as a father.

My dad plays a role in all of this. He has completed his stage as the father of five, with all of his children grown and married, and has commenced into his new, beloved role of *Paw-Paw*. You don't have to ask him if he likes having grandkids. All you have to do is watch the way he behaves around them. When my kids walk through the door of his house or into the room where he is, I say they have entered *the kingdom of yes*. Whatever they ask for, the answer is *yes, certainly, absolutely*, and *of course you can*. It's as though my father was saying to them, "Forget what your stuffy parents told you before you came. You are in *my* presence now, and I have given you the keys to the kingdom." I often wonder where this man was when I was growing up.

The answer, however humorous, is really rather profound if you think about it. The reason that my father has the opportunity to enjoy his grandchildren at this point in his life is because he took great care and responsibility in caring for his five children earlier in life. He successfully completed one chapter of life and has commenced with the next. It is the next logical and natural progression. You see, until you do what is required of you in one stage of life, you cannot fully enjoy the next. By completing his job as a father, my dad could embark on being a grandfather, and he soaks it up for all it's worth! After all, I assure you we made him earn it.

While this example may seem very simplistic, the fact is that too many people are unwilling to do what is required of them even at this basic level. They want the pleasures and joys of life to which they feel entitled, but not the ones that they have actually earned. Let's look at a few more examples.

People think that with four years of college under their belts, they deserve a secure, high-paying job with great benefits. They expect to receive a deposit to their bank accounts on payday, but they are not willing to take responsibility and produce more than they consume to work hard for their companies. Citizens feel that the government owes them some sort of utopian existence where every question is answered and every problem is solved. Yet they are not willing to stand up and be responsible to defend the freedom and liberty upon which this nation was built. Rather than confront the problems, they live to compromise.

When you stop to take a closer look at your life, you will clearly see that there is no easy street—not on any level. If you are going to build a life that you can enjoy, then you must make up your mind to earn it every day in some way. Again, consider the illustration regarding fathers and grandfathers.

There are many cases, unfortunately, in which fathers have abandoned their responsibilities concerning their children. This neglect causes them to be estranged from their children, thus disqualifying them from ever having the opportunity to enjoy a relationship with not only their children but also with their children's children. The deficient chapters of their lives hinder the current story from being the pleasant reality they once hoped for, all because they did not complete what they had embarked on—fatherhood. In failing to finish what they started by doing what is required of fathers, they forfeited the future. This principle can be illustrated over and over again with any number of situations and in almost every circumstance.

There are people who face this same issue concerning their physical health, just like those in fractured family relationships. The choices they made in one stage of life have not allowed them to commence enjoying today. Be it bad eating habits or lack of physical exercise or just plain laziness, the choices they made in the past encumber their next stage.

For others it might be financial choices. Rather than becoming responsible stewards, they buried themselves under mountains of debt and materialism. Now a weighed anchor hangs around their necks, and the life they are living is nothing like the life they had hoped for.

In Section 1 of this book I will show you that no matter the circumstance you find yourself in today, you are able to respond.

You can make a difference if you will become personally committed to doing so. It takes courage and commitment, but these two ingredients, combined with some genuine dedication, will give you all the strength you need to change the direction your life is going and give you the hope and future you desire. You can leave the past behind and not look back. Always remember: Yesterday is gone, tomorrow is beyond your reach, *but today is in your grasp*. What you do with it is up to you. If you handle it right, when today is complete, you will commence upon tomorrow with triumph instead of tragedy. The choice is yours.

Step 1.1

RESPOND BASED ON PRINCIPLE

I F YOU TRULY wish to make a change on anything great or small, you must always keep in mind that it begins and ends with you. Many people live life in reverse; they are always ready to tell us what is wrong with the big picture. These people have a bad case of what I call the "I'll tell you what you need to do" disease. They have the answers for everyone else's problem. They can solve all of the diffi-cult issues of life in one power lunch, but they can never seem to get things to add up in their own existence. It doesn't really matter what the issue is; they'll look you in the eyes with confidence and say, "I'll tell you what they need to do." The passionate monologue that follows usually sounds good, but it rarely produces results. I was taught that before you can address the change you want to see in someone else's life, you have to take account of the change you are willing to make in your own life. Maybe when I was younger it sounded like "Practice what you preach." While it may sound elementary, this principle has had a profound impact on me.

It's easy to get on your soapbox filled with passion and fire and tell others in a reverent tone how to live; it's altogether a different thing to live it. When you live it, it's a matter of principle, and principles endure long after the fire of passion burns out.

When responding to life, I highly recommend that you do so based on *principle* instead of *passion*. Passions are very fickle things at best and are famous for running hot and cold. One reason very few people make effective lasting change is because they seldom base their actions on solid principles, but rather let them be fueled by passion. Everywhere you turn you see lives that are driven by passion rather than ruled by principle.

The flames of uncontrolled passion can reduce the most established life into a pile of ashes. How many times have you seen the guy who has it all go down in flames because he based his choices on passion rather than live his life based on principle?

However, lives that are built on a foundation of principle will have stability that is able to endure the most volatile of times.

In 1981 when my father began supporting Israel and the Jewish community, it was not because of passion, but principle. As a man of the Word, it was required of him to do so. It was extremely controversial, often ridiculed, and even to this day heavily scrutinized, but still the results are impossible to deny and came as a matter of principle.

Consider Job, a man who experienced a tremendous amount of sudden changes. He saw all of his wealth, which had taken a lifetime of work and effort to amass, vanish in one day—along with all his children, whom he deeply loved and cherished, and his own personal health. Yet when the sun set on his tragedy and all that he held dear was laid to waste, from a foundation of principle he was able to say, "The Lord gave, and the Lord has taken away; blessed be the name of the Lord" (Job 1:21).

From observing my father's life of ministry to others, I could fill this book with stories of one personal tragedy after another, some of which would send chills running down your spine if you heard the details. The difference in the outcome of each is marked by those who responded to life's most challenging days with *principle* rather than letting their *passions* overtake them.

How do you live your life? Do you live it upon a solid foundation of principle or upon the volatile passion of the moment? If you live by principle, you're well on your way to being a difference maker. Not only are you on the road to your very own personal revolution, but also you can impact change in others as well. If you are planning to make a physical turnaround, no matter what resources you seek to assist you, no matter your circumstance, lasting change is a matter of principle; it will be the changes in physical principle that will actually revolutionize your health. Likewise, if it's a financial principle, it will be an economic turnaround. However, if your passion is in the driver's seat, then good luck, because I assure you, not even you know what you will do next.

One very simple illustration that I observed one evening at a friend's house demonstrates how simple and yet powerful this point can be in your life. We had finished dinner, and I was invited to sit in the living room for a visit and conversation while the hostess and her teenage children cleared the table and did the dishes. As the evening went on and the sound of dishes and silverware clattered in the sink, there was suddenly a sharp sound of something shattering, which rang out above every other noise. After a brief moment of tense silence, the noise in the kitchen carried on, and cleaning was back under way.

It was at this time my host said something that jumped out at me, and I have not forgotten it to this day. Sitting in the other room, not even able to see the commotion in the kitchen, he said, "My wife dropped that one."

I quickly asked him, "How can you tell?"

His response was both honest and sad. "She didn't yell at any of the kids."

The more I thought about it, the more it bothered me. Dropping a dish is an accident. As a matter of fact, if you have never done it, it simply means you don't do many dishes. This honest mistake could have been made by anyone, but in this particular home, if Mom made the mistake, no one said a word; but if one of the kids made the same mistake, then Mom was going to let them have it. Why? It was because the mother's passion dictated her behavior.

Remember that I said there are plenty of dictators in the world waiting for the chance to take control. Well, not all of them wear military uniforms and steal elections. Some of them are those personal emotions and behaviors that have total control over you.

If breaking a dish was a matter of principle, the moment the plate slipped out of her hand, she should have been held accountable for the misdeed. However, because it was not a matter of principle but just an honest mistake, no one made mention of it. Had someone else done the same, she would allow her personal dictator to explode with passion over the broken porcelain on the kitchen floor.

What alternate principle has more value to the quality of life in a home? It is the principle that the kids help Mom out around the house. Then, even though accidents happen, they can still graciously host a guest without the passion-driven idea that if the kids drop a dish, you're dead, and don't laugh if Mom does it—or at least not while she's still in the room. One principle brings a family together; the other drives them apart. One says, "Even if you make a mistake, I still love you and appreciate that you are trying and doing your part." The other says, "Don't you dare mess up."

I know that some of you are thinking, "Wow, all of this over a plate!" Not really; I only use the story to bring to light the fact that people are allowing their passions to dictate their behaviors, and they are yelling at each other about a lot more than just dirty dishes. In doing so, they are allowing their passions to drive them apart rather than allow their principles to pull them together.

Take a moment and consider how many areas of the world around you are totally polarized by passion. Two opposing sides, and both are devaluing the other and refusing any quarter or ounce of surrender because passion is on parade.

A conversation after dinner in the living room over a broken dish might be a small thing, but it was an object lesson that illustrated something my father asked me long ago: "Son, why do you do what you do?" Is it because it's the right thing to do no matter the circumstances or emotions you are dealing with, or is it because you allow your passions to dictate?

Principles are powerful. They will make men out of boys and instill a foundation in future generations that cannot be shaken. It takes courage to do what is right, no matter what and strength to keep passion under control at all cost. That doesn't mean you cannot be passionate about the things you love.

Consider my family. You can't be around the Hagees very long without knowing we are people filled with passion. We are the loudest at the Little League game, the most competitive on family game night, and don't even try to take us on in a golf match! Visit Cornerstone on Sunday, and for an hour and a half you will experience passion-filled moments—but it is *principle* that is in the driver's seat. Unless you live your life in proper order, you cannot expect to make progress and achieve a goal of any kind, because your passion will lead you astray. When you live your life in proper order, you can become passionate about your principles rather than be dictated by your passions.

As a husband and father, I have a number of principles for my home. First and foremost is that we honor the Lord God. Does that mean that we live perfect little halo-wearing lives? Hardly. I don't know a soul who does. What it does mean is that we strive to please Him in all that we do. This principle is something that we are passionate about as a family. It is why we go to church together and pray together. It is why we read the Word of God to our children and challenge them to memorize it and hide it in their hearts so that they can live lives that honor God.

We don't do it because it's popular or because everyone up and down the block is doing the same. We do it because it is a principle foundation of our lives that makes us who we are. We do it because one day I want to be a grandfather who has the opportunity to spoil my grandchildren in my very own *kingdom of yes*. I do it because rather than being the guy who sits in the corner of the restaurant filling the air with what others ought to say and do, I want to be the kind of person who, by setting an example with my own behavior and that of my family, inspires others to say, "I want to live like you."

It's how I was raised, and for me, it's a matter of principle to see my children do the same. This one truth can change your life. Principles enable you to become an example to others in a way that may change their lives too. They can lead you to a life of submission, which may be the missing ingredient to achieving your greatness and one that can lead you to the next step in your personal revolution. So, what drives you: principle or passion?

Take a moment before going on to the next step, and consider some principles that you might want to live by. As a guide for you, I have written three that I strive to achieve on a daily basis in my own life based on what my father taught me. You may want to write more, or you may want to list specific details that will help to create your personal prescription. Whether you choose to participate in the exercise of actually writing something down or simply take a moment or two to ponder what you see before you is up to you. What is important to note is that *principles have the power to turn around your personal life.* Any response you make to the world around you should be a matter of principle.

Step 1.1: Principles of Personal Responsibility

- Personal Principle 1: Invest more in others than you spend on yourself.

- Personal Principle 2: Live every day as if there is instant replay and your every move is going to be reviewed.

- Personal Principle 3: Be grateful for everything. Even the hard days have value.

Questions to Consider

1. Do I live my everyday life based on principle or passion?

_____

_____

2. Is there an area of my life where my passion is out of control?

   _____

   _____

3. What is one principle I can put into effect and live by, starting today?

   _____

   _____

Step 1.2

RESPONSIBLE PEOPLE ARE SUBMITTED PEOPLE

DON'T EVER UNDERESTIMATE the power of genuine humility and submission. Humility is a principle that everyone should live by. Unfortunately, passion often gets in the way, which leads to the exact opposite of humility and willing submission—humiliation and forced submission. Regardless, the truth remains that you will never know how powerful you can be until you willingly submit. Through each act of willing submission you will increase in your ability and power to truly change the world. My father submitted to the call of God on his life to preach the gospel at the age of seventeen. Fifty-four years later he has changed the world for hundreds of thousands of people.

Whether you realize it or not, everything lives in submission to something else. The sun lives in submission to the hours of the day and the orbit of the earth. It does not shine as it pleases; it shines in submission to the divine command under which it has lived since the beginning. The oceans are in submission to the tides and currents, hemmed in by the shore that surrounds them on all sides. Your natural life is lived in submission to the laws of nature in the world around you. As much as you might wish you could rebel against the law of gravity, as long as you are in this earth's atmosphere, you are submitted to its pull. Try as you might to defy it, if you jump off a building one hundred times, each and every time a fall will result.

Your civil life is lived in submission to the laws of the municipality where you live. The citizenship of your nationality will determine which flag and constitution you are submitted to in the world. The relationships you maintain in your personal life will determine the level of submission you have to others. For example, in my own life, as a son I am submitted to the leadership of my father, as a husband I am submitted to the needs of my wife, and as a father I am submitted to the needs of my children. In my role as a pastor, I am submitted to the calling that God has placed on me and to the church where He has ordained me to serve, and as His child I am submitted to His lordship in every area of my life.

The joy of submission is this: The amount of submission you are willing to live under will determine the level of success you can achieve. The more capable the leader you choose to submit to, the greater quality of life you will enjoy. However, in our modern way of thinking, submission is a dirty word. It represents, to those who do not truly understand it, confinement and hindrance, which are disablers rather than enablers.

As a matter of fact, I would be willing to bet that many of you reading this book would think that submission is the exact opposite of what this volatile world needs in order to see real change. On the contrary, no change is successful without submission to the cause.

Consider the Revolutionary War that led to the birth of this nation and changed the world. Those we know as the Founding Fathers submitted themselves to the needs of the oppressed citizens who were living under the tyranny of the royals. They submitted themselves to the point that they pledged their lives, their fortunes, and their sacred honor. Some lost their lives, others lost their fortunes, but each kept his honor. By their sacrifice they not only purchased freedom for their generation, but they also established a standard of liberty for future generations to enjoy all over the globe today. Their revolution was not so much about rebelling against the leadership of King George, but rather in them submitting themselves to the defense of freedom.

From their example we see that the greater the cause, the greater the sacrifice that's required, and the greater the sacrifice, the greater the success. If you are looking for a personal revolution to begin in your own life, then you are going to have to submit yourself to the cause. This requires a great amount of personal responsibility. Simply put, you must run *to* responsibility rather than *from* it. This is a life lesson my father taught me. However, today's society has become experts in passing on the blame and finger-pointing. It is in our nature to do so.

The very first time man had the opportunity to blame someone else, he did. After Adam ate the fruit and was asked to give an explanation as to why he had directly disobeyed, his response was, "It's not my fault. It's this woman that You gave me." (See Genesis 3:12.) With that statement he was actually pointing the finger in two directions. In essence, Adam was saying, "I didn't do it; she did—and by the way, she wouldn't be here to mess things up if You had not brought her to me."

There are a lot of people who behave the same way today. When they are held accountable for the outcome of their situations, they have a long list of people who are to blame, but they are never on the list. They may not recognize it, but in their unending litany of whining, in effect they are all too often putting the blame on God. They think they can't possibly be at fault or the cause behind their crisis. It must be the government, the economy, the environment, my neighbor, my teacher, the preacher, my spouse, my egomaniacal boss, anyone and anything but me. Then they throw in the ever pathetic "I just don't know why God lets these things happen." They actually behave as if the sovereign God fell asleep at the wheel and unknowingly brought them to this end. With that one line, just like Adam, they say, "Lord, it's as much Your fault as everyone else's, but it isn't mine!"

Submission to personal responsibility will change all of that.

First, submission willingly does what is required by the given authority it is under. It's not a matter of understanding; it's a matter of obedience. The sooner you grasp this truth, the easier your life will be. I could fill a library full of reference books with the things that I don't understand. But it is the things that I obey that determine the quality of my life and shape my destiny.

As a child growing up, it was very obvious that obedience had a direct relationship on my quality of life in the house. The lines were clear and the principles upheld always without wavering. From this experience of growing up in my house, I learned the connection between relationship and responsibility. For example, in my relationship with God I am responsible to live a life of faith and trust in obedience to His Word. I am responsible for my actions; He is responsible for the outcome. Human nature is so impatient that we often begin to make sudden and impulsive changes because we are not at all pleased with our immediate outcome. It's important to remember that results take time, and if you do your part, the results will come. Consider this Scripture verse: "Your ears will hear a voice behind you, saying, 'This is the way; walk in it'" (Isaiah 30:21, NIV).

That particular verse is referencing our relationship with God, who is also our Shepherd. We are often referred to as "the sheep of His pasture." If you have ever observed sheep with their shepherd, the sheep are following him, not the other way around. The sheep are following him because they are so dependent and needy upon him to lead them to food, water, and shelter and to keep an eye out for danger. Consider this: if we are the sheep, and the voice of the Shepherd is behind us, who is out of place? This verse is describing sheep who have wandered out on their own in search of their own provision. When they have not found what they are looking for, the gentle Shepherd is there to say, "Hey, this way; you missed a turn back here." When you willingly submit to the Shepherd, He takes care of the results. Your responsibility is just to obey and follow.

By willingly submitting to authority, you are free to enjoy the benefits that your leader can provide. For example, growing up in my home as a child, I was one of five who had the opportunity to enjoy the benefits and blessings that my parents could provide. All I had to do was submit. I was blessed by Mom preparing the meals, keeping the house, doing laundry, and watching after our well-being. I was blessed by Dad paying the mortgage, keeping the lights on and the water running, and providing every opportunity to succeed and enjoy life. It was great! When I was the child in their home, I didn't have to pay one bill, fix one meal, or make any hard choices. They were the leaders, and that was their job. All I had to do was obey, grow up, and take advantage of the opportunities that they were able to provide. Now that I am the dad and no longer under my parent's roof, I have the bills and my kids enjoy the food. The answers to the hard questions fall on me.

Regarding whether or not I would willingly submit, I remember one particular day when I had to cross a bridge. It was indeed a decision that shaped my life from that day to this one, and all my future days that God gives me the grace to live. Here are the details.

I had just graduated from high school and was ninety days away from leaving for college. My father, knowing that I had made it clear I wanted to be in the ministry, told me that he wanted me to preach the final Sunday night in July before I left for the university. Having all summer to prepare my message, I put all I had into the effort. I called down fire, mixed with thunder and lighting, mentally prepared for the masses that would swoon under the anointing. When all was said and done, I had thirty-five pages of pulpit perfection! (A forty-five-minute sermon is only eighteen to twenty pages more or less.) Thirty-five pages in the hands of a seventeen-year-old is a recipe for disaster.

The moment had finally come for me to present my manuscript to my father, and I knew this would be the moment that he would truly recognize the raw brilliance that stood before him. Much to my shock and dismay, he read the title, text, and first paragraph of my introduction and said the only words I would hear him say for the next hour and half, "Son, go get my red pen!"

What? *The red pen?* Surely I misunderstood him; there was no need for a red pen to be used to make corrections. This masterpiece was perfect. Ninety minutes later, he had reduced thirty-five pages into two three-sentence paragraphs and then spoke these words: "Those two paragraphs are worth keeping because they come from the Bible; the rest of that stuff comes from you, and people who are hurting and searching for answers don't come to church to hear from you. They come to hear the Word. You can keep what's circled, but you need to try again."

I was devastated. My ego was crushed. I wasn't humbled; I was humiliated. I walked back into the study of our home, and I began to build my argument. I threw the pages lined and crossed over with red ink in the trash can and started calling on the courage to walk back into my father's bedroom and tell him why he was so very wrong. Just as I was getting up from the desk to ring the bell on round two, a *still, small voice* asked this question, and it changed my life forever: "Is this where your ministry will end?" "*What?*" I thought. "Where in the world did that come from?"

Then I looked down into the trash can where I had thrown my manuscript. There, on those pages, were not the red lines of my worst critic, but the loving leadership of my biggest fan. Suddenly, I thought about who it was who had taken the time to read my very first sermon. How many other preachers, who had been in the ministry a lot longer than I had been, who had accomplished so much more than I had, would have given anything to have the opportunity for John Hagee to read and critique a sermon of theirs? I was not unappreciated and abused; I was privileged and loved. If I would willingly submit to his leadership and instruction, then years of wisdom would be made accessible to me. If I decided to search for another opinion, one that might stroke my ego and puff up my pride instead of empower me to become the minister I needed to be, then I would have faced the humiliation of failure my first time in the pulpit.

Thankfully, I paid attention to the still, small voice. I may not have understood in that moment all that hung in the balance, but I obeyed what my earthly father and heavenly Father were leading me to do—and I can assure you, beyond any shadow of a doubt, doing so has truly revolutionized my young life. I pulled the manuscript out of the trash and did as I was told. I started over and asked for lots of help along the way. Today that manuscript—all sixteen pages of it—hangs framed in my office at the church. It hangs as a personal reminder not only of the last Sunday night in July 1996 but also of the moment I truly came to understand the power you can possess when you willingly submit.

Section 1.2: Responsible People
Are Submitted People

- The greater the level of submission, the greater the level of success.

- Submit to responsibility rather than run from it.

- You are responsible for your actions. The leader you have submitted to is responsible for the results.

Questions to Consider

1. Am I willingly submitted to the cause and ready to obey, even if I don't understand?

_____

_____

2. Am I out in front of the leader and ignoring the *still, small voice* behind me?

_____

_____

3. In what areas of my life do I risk humiliation and forced submission if I do not take action and get them back under control now?

_____

_____

Step 1.3

PERSONALLY DECLARE WAR ON THE STATUS QUO

ONE MESSAGE MY father has driven home to all who know him is the attitude and spirit of excellence. I was taught, "Do it well and with all you've got, or don't do it at all!" If your desire is truly to make a difference in this world, you must wage war on mediocrity.

Having said that, know that there is no such thing in life as true equality. There never has been, and there never will be. As a matter of fact, to try and force equality is against the laws of nature. As humans, each of us was designed with unique individuality. Genesis 1:27 reads, "Male and female He created them." There is a difference, and I for one thank God for it each and every day. Our Creator may love us equally, but we are not equals in physical ability or emotional chemistry or any other natural form of measure. To try and force the issue is contrary to nature.

I have a daughter, and from the day she could walk and talk, she has loved to play house, dress up, wear makeup, and play *mommy*. At the age of five, she can go on and on with my wife about what they are going to wear or the things they are going to decorate or which color accessories match which outfit. On the other hand, my four-year-old son loves trucks, trains, guns, playing rough, and getting dirty. As their dad, I say, "Thank heaven for little girls, and hallelujah for little boys."

I bring this up because we, as a society, have been duped into believing that through some system of social standard we can create equality for any and everything. This is just not true, and it will never be achieved. The only thing that can and should be equally given to all men and women everywhere is the opportunity to make choices. Choose the God you will worship. Choose whether or not you will work and earn a living or be lazy and starve to death. Choose to be a blessing in the lives of others or selfishly exist only for yourself.

The opportunity to choose is the only real *equal opportunity* you will ever have. Other than that, the differences in your life that set you apart from the rest of the world are up to you. That is why you have to declare war on the status quo and refuse to settle for mediocre or average. In order to make a real difference physically, professionally, personally, or in any other area, you must first decide to stop measuring your success or failure by the standards set by the guy across the street and begin looking within yourself.

Where do you draw the line, and by what measure do you gauge success or failure? I recommend the ultimate measuring stick, the Word of God. Within the pages of this sacred text are the standards of life that set those who live by them far apart from the rest of the world. The ungodly will look at the quality of life you live and be envious that they are not the ones receiving the blessings. The Bible, from cover to cover, speaks of people who live lives that are set apart. Those who follow biblical standards are distinguished from others around them, as the "the head and not the tail…above only, and not be beneath" (Deuteronomy 28:13). There isn't much equality rhetoric in that.

Once you have declared war on the status quo, you must begin to go on the offensive by doing just a little bit more to be a little bit better every day. Why such little steps? Because nobody gets there in a day, but doing just a little bit more makes a great deal of difference over time.

Physically, the way you increase in strength is by progressively lifting heavier weights. However, if you stayed at the same weight level because you were unwilling to advance, then eventually you would stagnate and not achieve the improvement you wanted in your physical body. Professionally, if you declare war on the status quo, you can make the kind of difference in your office that revolutionizes your workplace because you are willing to do what others aren't. You might say, "Yeah, well, but these are some high standards." I challenge you to see the standards set before you as hurdles that you can jump in order to reach the winner's circle—not as an iron ceiling that is impossible to get beyond.

Personally, it is never too late to better yourself. You can change your future one day at a time, if you are willing to take the necessary steps to create the change. Just because it was good enough for the last guy doesn't mean it's good enough for you. The only standard you are held to is the one by which you are willing to live. Many times we like to talk about the unnatural amount of talent that people of great achievement possess. We look at our sports heroes and great musical talents and talk about them as if in some way they are from another planet, abnormal beings. However, a closer look reveals that while they do have a measure of talent, the best and brightest are the ones who are willing to work the hardest and set themselves apart from the pack. It is the musician who practices for hours … the athlete who drills, drills, and drills until exhaustion has set in and then drills again. It is the vocalist who practices the placement of every note until he is confident he has mastered the melody and is ready to sing the song. It is the businessman who has attempted to succeed at nine great ideas and failed, and who, in spite of his previous setbacks, is still courageous enough to try again. These are just some examples of people who are willing to do what it takes to be set apart; there is no reason that you cannot be numbered among them.

Making the determination to reach a little deeper, try a little harder, and not stop until you have achieved the goal you set out to reach will have your life turned around and headed in the right direction. The moment you make up your mind that the status quo may be good enough for some, but it's just not good enough for you, then you can be confident that things in your future are destined to change.

Step 1.3: My Personal Declaration of War

- I will not settle for average; I am better than that.

- I will discover the difference that doing a little more every day can make.

- I will not allow the standards of my life to be determined by those around me, but rather determined by what God has intended for me.

Questions to Consider

1. When is the last time I consistently tried to do a little better each and every day?

   _____

   _____

2. What areas of my life are suffering in quality from a status quo mentality?

   _____

   _____

3. What standards do I need to overcome in order to revolutionize my future?

   _____

   _____

Step 1.4

BE THANKFUL FOR TODAY AND PREPARED FOR TOMORROW

I F I HEARD it once, I heard it a thousand times: "Son, always hope for the best; always be prepared for the worst." This principle is so crucial to being able to make a response to the drastic changes of life that I would be remiss if I didn't share it with you now. It's not a matter of overwhelming pessimism or far-reaching optimism; it's a matter of realism and gratitude for all that you have and don't deserve.

In this life there are indeed no guarantees. The way you approach this truth is entirely up to you, but before you make your decision, consider how your perspective will impact the future quality of your life. Some say there are no guarantees, so grab all you can and take whatever you can get, because tomorrow it may be gone. This approach is probably more common than we would like to admit and is based upon a very serious personal defect: greed. When you hope for the best, you do not create the need or desire to hoard your resources or lay claim to what is not yours.

The concept of scarcity—what you see before you today may not be there tomorrow—leads to a *greed mentality* that convinces you to get it while the getting is good, even if you don't need it right now. That is why the discount and bulk supermarkets are so popular. You don't need five gallons of mayonnaise and fifty pounds of pickles, but it's on sale today, so you figure you can store it until the end of the decade— and you rent a storage unit across town to hold the things that won't fit in the pantry because you believe it's better to buy two cases of each!

This kind of hoarding doesn't only occur in the pantry. It happens financially and emotionally and can destroy lives and relationships. Financially, people see an uncertain economic environment, and rather than manage their resources conservatively and with a greater level of stewardship, they shut down all together. They put everything away in the coffee can and in the mattress. They keep currency from moving and in effect only add to the economic problem rather than solve it.

Personal history plays a definite role in this matter as well. For example, my grandparents, like many others in their generation, lived through the economic depression of the late twenties and thirties in the last century. It created such a mind-set in my grandfather that up to his last day on earth, he would still say, "Squeeze a nickel until the buffalo cries." I recall my father telling me that on one occasion my grandfather joined some of the men in their church for a fishing trip to the Texas coast. The plan was to meet at a state park, camp for the night, and then get up and fish in the morning. After a long drive, my grandfather arrived at the park entrance and was told, like everyone else had been, that there was a two-dollar admission charge. You could always tell how my grandfather was going to react based on how tight he set his jaw. The thought that he was required to pay to enter a state park that his tax dollars had already paid for caused him to set his jaw tight and clinch his teeth. He refused, basing his argument on the fact that, "I have already paid for this property, and I am not going to give twice to get into what is already mine." He turned his car around and drove back to Houston because the *scarcity mentality* stood in the way of his enjoying life.

While to some extent this may sound logical, to another extent consider what the mind-set really cost him. Over a sum of eight quarters, he forfeited the opportunity to enjoy an evening with fellow men of God and to create pleasant memories of fishing with his son.

People do the same thing emotionally. They go through an emotional great depression. They endure hard times brought on, in many cases, by circumstances out of their control, and the end result is they refuse to invest themselves in others from that point forward. They refuse to trust because at some point in the past they have been betrayed. They refuse to celebrate because they fear that disaster may be waiting around the next corner. Due to emotionally hoarding themselves in this way, they become isolated and live a life that is void of many of the real joys God intended every life to have. Rather than hope for the best, they expect the worst, and it greatly impacts their ability to enjoy life.

There are no guarantees, so you can either invest yourself in worrying about what may or may not be available tomorrow, or you can be grateful for what you have today. The best way to enjoy life is to live it with gratitude. This approach is opposite to the concept of scarcity, which can lead to greed. The gratitude mind-set understands that the blessings you enjoy were brought into your life by the hand of God, and the greatest thing you can do to demonstrate your appreciation is to be thankful for what He has done and trust Him to provide for you in the future. Your hope for tomorrow is in a God who is the same yesterday, today, and forever.

While hoping for the best enables you to enjoy the life you live, it's crucial that you also take the time to be prepared for whatever may be ahead. The Book of Proverbs says, "A prudent man foresees evil and hides himself; the simple pass on and are punished" (Proverbs 27:12). When it comes to preparing for your future, hide yourself—not in fear but in confidence that the shadow of the wings of the Lord God is well able to protect you.

We have thunderstorms in South Texas that, at times, can get to be rather exciting. They cause the wind to suddenly gust and lightning to crack as it crashes to the ground. They can drop so much water in such a short period of time that flash floods are common and in some areas fatal. When these violent storms come, I do not run under the nearest bush and cower and tremble and pray that I make it through. I simply go into my house, which is built on a solid foundation with sturdy walls and a proper roof, and wait until the storm passes by. I am not hiding myself in fear; I am hiding myself in confidence knowing that my chosen shelter is more than able to endure the weather outside.

There is no shortage of hard times that we must endure while we live in this world. There are financial storms that have the best and the brightest financial minds scratching their heads. There are physical pandemics that no matter how hard you try to avoid them, they still seem to be unavoidable. There is an emotional heaviness and frustration that has people searching for joy and peace in a world that seems to be falling apart.

The best place to find yourself in the midst of any one of these storms is sheltered in the refuge of God's unchanging hand. He is the one who enabled you to enjoy today, and He will be the One to sustain you tomorrow. That's why gratitude will get you a lot further than greed every time. The Bible tells us, "In everything give thanks" (1 Thessalonians 5:18).

Gratitude is the key that releases the supernatural power of God in your life. The Bible says, "Be thankful to Him, and bless His name" (Psalm 100:4). Gratitude is the attitude that will revolutionize your outlook on everything. Knowing that the God of heaven is watching over you here on Earth will enable you to lie down and rest at night with the confidence that He is far too wise to be mistaken, entirely too powerful to be overtaken, and way too loving to be unkind.

Your ability to be grateful is not determined by your circumstance; it is a matter of choice. You either *decide* to enjoy everything that you can about the moment you are living in, or you *refuse* to. It's up to you. The best way to be thankful for today and prepare for tomorrow is to understand you are what you believe in your heart yourself to be. Consider Joseph. There were a number of days in his life when he appeared to others to be far less than the ruler his dream had depicted, but nevertheless, he never lost sight of what the Lord had shown him, and he was able to achieve his destiny.

King Solomon, who was the wisest man on the face of the earth, said, "For as he thinks in his heart, so is he" (Proverbs 23:7). When building your life on principle, you have to start by clearly understanding who you are and where your ability comes from. You have to stop saying, "I can't," and start believing, "I can do all things through Christ who strengthens me" (Philippians 4:13). Get the word *if* out of your vocabulary, and start saying, "With God's help and by His grace, I will." Stop listening to the mediocre minds around you, and stay focused on the magnificent thought that "all things are possible to him who believes" (Mark 9:23).

You can change your life forever the moment you begin to believe. Whatever the mind can believe, it can achieve. You will never start believing anything good about your tomorrows until you become thankful for what you have today.

If you reject the opportunity to be grateful, you embrace the forces of doubt and depression that will become dreaded dictators in your life. You will walk around with the mind-set "Nothing good will ever happen to me." I will be the first to tell you, you're right. No matter how big the blessing, with a self-centered, greed-driven attitude you will always be a victim of your circumstances. It won't matter how sweet life is to you; you'll always choose to eat the sour grapes.

What you have today is a gift from God. What you do with it is your gift to Him. Unwrap the gift with gratitude, and make it a down payment on tomorrow. Whimpering and whining about what you wish life would be is a waste of time and takes up way too much energy. Being responsible for the attitude that you have, and doing the work that needs to be done to make your life and the lives of others better, is not only gratifying, but it also energizes you for the challenges you will face in the future.

Thank God every day as if it was your last time to ever give thanks. Far too many people postpone being thankful until everything is perfect. If that's what you are waiting on, it will never happen. Be thankful right now, because today is the best day of your life.

Well, what about tomorrow? Leave that up to the One who holds tomorrow. Be thankful for the shelter you have, which protects from the storms. Be grateful for the provision that has been made available to you today, and refuse to allow doubt, depression, and scarcity to cause you to worry about what might happen tomorrow. If you truly want to live a life of abundance, stop toiling over the accumulation of material possessions, and start enjoying the possessions that you have been blessed with *right now*.

Gratitude will turn your life around faster than any other thing, because it will cause you to focus on what is truly important. This life is made up of opportunities—you will choose them or refuse to take them. If you are not thankful for today and prepared for tomorrow, you will greatly hinder your ability to make quality decisions. You will be distracted from your purpose and stop reaching for your destiny. The only way to focus on what is clearly in front of you is to be grateful for what you have been given. Understand where it came from, and trust that your source will not fail you in the future. In a world that has mastered the art of complaint and misery, gratitude can start a revolution. Let that turnaround happen in you.

Step 1.4: The Things I Am Truly Thankful For

- Physical strength

- Love and support of friends and family

- Redemption, grace, and mercy

- Provision, protection, and peace of mind

Questions to Consider

1. Do I operate from a mentality of scarcity in the resources of this world or in the abundance of my God?

_____

_____

2. What are the ten things that I will be thankful for each and every day?

_____

_____

3. Whose life can I change by demonstrating gratitude toward that person and others?

_____

_____

Step 1.5

GENEROUSLY INVEST IN OTHERS

BY NOW I believe it is easier for you to see that these steps of personal responsibility are very much dependent upon each other.

Unless your life is ruled by principle, you will not be able to willingly submit when everything inside of you wants to do the opposite. Unless you are willingly submitted to your God-appointed leadership, you will not have the self-discipline to declare war on the status quo. In a world that is centered on cynicism and selfish ambition, you will not be able to be thankful for today and prepare for tomorrow unless you have separated yourself from the average pessimist. And, without gratitude, you will not be able to achieve the next step, step five, which is to generously invest in others.

All of my life I have watched my father generously invest himself in others. It began with his children and family, extended to his church members, then his community, and from there to the nation and the world. It didn't happen with his own well-being and desire at the forefront; it came as a result of considering what he wanted to see in the lives of others and then seeing if he could play a role in bringing it to pass. Question: Do you regularly invest yourself in others?

People immediately run to the thought of financial capital when the topic of investment is brought up. They begin to analyze dollars given versus dividends received and at what rate recoupment can be expected. All of that lingo and jargon has value in the boardroom of business; however, it is all but bankrupt when it comes to changing your life.

However, take a moment to consider the capital you have to invest in the lives of others and truly think about all you possess in your portfolio. You can make an investment of time, a kind word, a warm embrace, a card, letter, or e-mail that reminds someone you are thinking of them. The return on these investments is not measured in balance sheets and income statements but in the smile that you put on someone else's face and the one that you wear on your own.

When I was a child, I never considered for a moment what we as a family had or didn't have compared to those whom we knew, because I truly had all that I needed. I had a father who invested a tremendous amount of time in me and a mother who watched over my every need. I am challenged by their example to do as much, if not more, for my own children because of the investment my parents made in me. It has inspired me to invest myself not only in the lives of my children but also in the lives of others.

My father was the dad who never missed a game and did his best to always make it to practice. That took a great deal of investment. If he had given me a savings bond at the end of every season and said, "Here is what I earned for you while you were playing baseball," I would have looked at that piece of paper with resentment, because the most beloved memory of my life is the fact that he took the time to be there.

Not much has changed; I still very much cherish his presence. Those who know me well know that I love the outdoors. I have had a passion for hunting and fishing, horsemanship and ranching since I could walk. When I was eight years old, I began to ask my father if he and I could go on an elk hunt. Now, to help you understand the size of this request, you first must understand that if you live in Texas, hunting elk means you have to leave the state, and when you are Pastor Hagee, you live by a very strict law that states traveling over a weekend is rarely—if ever—done. The likelihood of being out of state and in the woods on a Sunday was nearly impossible. Still, being the persistent person that I am, each and every fall as the season approached, I would ask. Every fall the answer would be the same: *someday*.

Over the years, from time to time my father would offer me the opportunity to go on an elk adventure without him. He would say, "I know some folks who are going on an elk hunt. Why don't you go with them?" Every time I would refuse, because it wasn't so much about the hunt as it was about whom I would be hunting with—my dad. I would respond, "You know, I may have the opportunity someday to hunt all over the world, but I want the memory of my first elk hunt to be just as precious as the memory of my first deer hunt, which means I have to go with you." For the better part of fifteen years we had the conversation time and again.

Then finally on Christmas Day 2006 I received a card informing me that we—Dad and I—had an appointment for an elk hunt that following fall in the state of Idaho. It wasn't the actual journey that filled me with excitement; it was the fact that I would be going with him. By the way, we left on a Monday and were back on Friday—in time for church the following Sunday. It took some effort and patience, but he found a way to invest his time in my life.

You never know how it's going to pay off, but believe me it will. I have seen it over and over again. You may invest yourself in any number of ways and may never know when or how it will come back. Second Corinthians 9:6 says, "He who sows sparingly will also reap sparingly, and he who sows bountifully will also reap bountifully." It is possible to draw the conclusion that this verse relates only to finances, but it is truly much deeper than that.

Take a moment and consider the relationship between the amount of seed planted and the expected harvest. If you scatter only a few seeds in the ground, you cannot expect the barn to burst when it's harvest time. Likewise, if you don't invest yourself generously in the lives of others, you cannot expect them to invest themselves in you when you need it, and believe me, sooner or later you will need others. If you want to receive more, then you have to give more, and it really doesn't matter where you are looking for that return—the truth applies in all situations.

If you want to receive kindness and consideration from others, you first have to generously give kindness and consideration to them. If you want friendship, be a friend. If you want love, give love. If you want others to bring you joy, then you must be the kind of person who brings them joy.

The personal investment of your life into the lives of others is one of the most powerful investments you can make. It will not only change the lives of those you invest in, but it will also revolutionize your own. Years ago I met a local businessman in the San Antonio area who was truly one of the hardest-working people I had ever met. He was honest, straightforward, a no-nonsense kind of guy, and very likeable, whether you worked with him or not. After getting to know him a little better, it became very clear why he worked as hard as he did. His only son was debilitated with a horrific muscular disease that would cause him to grow progressively weaker over time and eventually lead to his demise. The force that drove this man was the hunger of a father to give his son every opportunity to enjoy each day of his life—no matter how limited their time together would be. The irony, and in some ways the cruelty, of the tragic situation was that in order to earn the income to take care of his son and spend time with the boy, the man had to work almost day and night.

His unending effort led to great financial results but limited his free time. Then one day he made an investment in someone else, and it changed everything. This businessman heard about another man who had fallen on hard times. Like many who find themselves in this situation, the man with his back against the wall owed more than he could afford to pay. He truly had no foreseeable way of appeasing his creditors. This dire situation was caused not by any poor choice of his own but by the unethical behavior of others who had taken what wasn't theirs and left this innocent man holding the bill without the resources to settle. Unfortunately, there are times the written law does not keep dishonest people from harming the innocent.

After becoming familiar with the situation, the businessman and father of the invalid boy called the man who had fallen on hard times to his office. He informed the man who was facing financial ruin that he had checked on the situation with his creditors and knew that he was not at fault, even though he was the responsible party. He also told him that he had found out how much he owed, a sum of more than a half million dollars. After bringing all of this to light, the businessman opened his desk drawer, pulled out his checkbook, and wrote the man a personal check for the amount he owed, plus some to help him get a new start. He said, "All I ask in return is that if you ever have the chance to help someone else out someday, that you would do the same."

Instantly the man who was the beneficiary of this generosity replied, "The person I'd like to help out is you." Now you might think that someone who could cut such a large check from his personal account wouldn't need any help, but the contrary was true.

The recipient of the funds said, "I am aware of the situation that you have with your son and how much you wish you could spend time with him. I also know that you are not able to do so because of the demands of your business. I will come to work for you for free to enable you to enjoy every day that you can with your child at home." The agreement was made, and the father has been at home with his son every day for the last two years. Meanwhile, the business has grown even larger with the new *manager,* and both men found a way to generously invest in one another and meet their most desperate needs. It is so true: *with the same measure that you sow, you shall reap.*

When you sow, do it because you are a giver and not because you are looking for a return. Do it joyfully even if there is no promise of a payback. Remember, you are not responsible for the results, merely your actions. What you give is up to you. A kind word spoken at the right time may be the priceless possession that a downhearted person needs. It may not seem like the most efficient thing to do with your time, but hours spent with friends and loved ones are never wasted. If you give properly, you will empower others to do the same. If you give as a means of control, then you have become a dictator, and it is only a matter of time before you find yourself facing revolt from those you are trying to control.

If you never allow the "what's in it for me" mentality to enter your mind, then you will be blessed in what you give each and every time. When you watch out for others, they begin to watch out for you. That requires a great deal of self-sacrifice, which, at times, is considered a novelty but is truly essential to making a difference in your life as well as the lives of others. The rewards of generosity far outweigh the cost and may be exactly what your life has been missing up to this point. If you have lived life generously and sown good seed, then get ready for harvest time! It's the only natural thing that can happen. By sowing before you needed to reap, you have prepared yourself for future success. If you have yet to sow, there is no better time to start than right now.

Step 1.5: Things I Can Invest in Others

- Kindness: I can give someone the benefit of the doubt rather than take them for granted.

- Joy: There is a terrible deficit in the amount of joy in the world today. This is something I can change.

- Hope: No matter what I give—finances, time, consideration, kindness—it should always cultivate hope in the lives of those who receive it.

Questions to Consider

1. When I give, why do I give? Is it for the return or for the joy of giving?

_____

_____

2. Is my giving empowering or enabling others to succeed?

   _____

   _____

3. Do I give to see others advance or to try and gain control?

   _____

   _____

Step 1.6

YOU MAY LOSE A BATTLE, BUT DON'T LOSE THE WAR

I N MY FATHER'S office at home sits a figurine I gave him for Father's Day when I was ten. There are two images portrayed on the same pedestal. One is a young boy in his Little League uniform with his hands raised in triumph, and the expression on his face is a reflection of the joy of success. Sitting next to the boy is the same figure with his hands on his knees, eyes fixed on the ground, and defeat all over his face. The work is called, "Sometimes you win, and sometimes you lose." The reasons I thought it was an appropriate piece for Father's Day are:

1. At ten, I was immersed in Little League.

2. My father made me memorize a phrase we repeat to each other even today: "Sometimes you get the bear, and sometimes the bear gets you."

It's a simple reminder that you don't hit a home run every time you step up to the plate, nor do you always strike out. Success and failure in life are not always measured by wins and losses but, in many cases, by the fact that you tried. If you quit because the results were less than you wanted them to be, then you are the loser indeed; but if you refuse to quit, when the conflict is over you will be the kid with your hands in the air. There are no limits for the one who refuses to quit. Therefore, as long as you are breathing, stay in the fight. All of my life I have heard my father preach and have watched him live by this motto.

One of his favorite illustrations of never quitting is a quote from Sir Winston Churchill: "The nose of a bulldog has been slanted backwards so he can breathe without letting go."[1] On many occasions I have heard my father make this statement from the pulpit, and by the very expression on his face, I can see in the theater of my mind a tenacious little dog clenching down with all of his might. The one who refuses to give up is the one who defies the dictators and achieves his destiny. You may lose a battle, but don't lose the war. Be aware that you will live to fight another day.

Without a doubt failure is an experience common to all of us. It will define you, or you will define it. Not achieving an intended outcome will either crush you or cause you to rise to the occasion as you refocus your sights to reach for greatness. The battlefield of the mind is the most important battlefront you will ever fight on. If you can change your mind and control your thoughts, you can change your world. If you allow the world to infect your mind with the poison of bitterness and resentment, you will be defeated before you even start. Remember this: Not everything you do will turn out like you expect, but no can keep you from trying again. If you make up your mind to become the hammer that refuses to quit pounding, sooner or later the rock will crack and the breakthrough will come.

If you declare war on the status quo and invest yourself generously in the lives of others, understand that sooner or later those you have invested in will disappoint you. Understand that when the attitudes of average and mediocre try to pull you down, don't consider it a strange thing; it is perfectly normal, and others have been where you are. What matters is that you will continue to declare war on the status quo and continue to invest in other people's lives no matter the outcome.

Trouble and strife do not mean that you have been forsaken; they mean that you are human. If you are willing to allow trouble to run its course, you will find that it strengthens you, and the resistance it provides will help to develop what was lacking within you. When the battle is finally over and the victory comes, you'll look back and say, like those who have gone before you, "It was good for me that I had been afflicted." (See Psalm 119:71.) We live in a world that craves comfort no matter what. I recommend you become uncomfortable—it can afford you the opportunity to achieve success.

Pay Attention

One of the greatest things you can do to assist yourself in this time of struggle and strife is to pay attention, because paying attention pays off. I suggest you pay attention in four areas. They are in no particular order, and you may even want to add to the list, but these are things I see people overlook on a very regular basis when they should be paying attention.

First, *pay attention to those who are successful.* They say that the greatest form of flattery is imitation. Therefore find someone who has achieved what you are trying to do and imitate that person's behavior. Believe me, it is easier said than done. One of the greatest challenges is finding someone who is truly successful rather than someone who just appears to be. The appearance of success is a lot more common than the real thing. Once you do find someone who is worth imitating, you soon discover that if it was as easy as they made it look, everyone would do it.

Second, *pay attention to those who fail.* In many cases you can learn so much more from the mistakes of others than you can from their successes. When you pay attention to those who fail, do not do it from a position of judgment, because you may very well find yourself at the center of the same situation some day. Do it out of respect for who they are, your fellow man, and the fact that they were indeed courageous enough to try while others were too afraid to even make that attempt.

Third, *pay attention to your tendencies.* We are all creatures of habit, and whether they are good or bad, our habits and tendencies greatly impact our outcome. It really doesn't matter who you are or what you do, but to some extent all of us have a certain way of doing things. No two chefs make the same dish exactly alike. They each place their own personal flare to it. The same is true of musicians and writers, builders and craftsmen. Our uniqueness is what makes us who we are. That being said, it is important to understand that your uniqueness can become your weakness if you do not pay attention to it.

For example, certain people tend to be sensitive; others are direct. If you are not aware of your tendency, and you do not pay attention to the person you are dealing with, you can create more problems than you can solve. I know people who make others feel uncomfortable when they walk into a room. It is because their tendency is to stay focused on a project, which keeps their mind a million miles away. In turn, it makes those in their presence feel as if they are unwelcomed or, worse yet, insignificant. This can lead to the alienation of relationships. Soon people start saying things like: "He's just not that friendly or personable," or "I don't think he likes me." That's not it at all; he is simply not paying attention to his tendency.

Finally, and maybe most importantly, *pay attention to your enemies.* They are very real and will do everything in their power to destroy you. Identify them, and do not hesitate to confront them. Refuse to allow them to become dictators who rule over you. Let them know by your deliberate and carefully thought-out actions that you have done your homework, you have paid attention, and you are not afraid to achieve success. And just when they think they have figured you out because they have paid attention to your tendencies, change it up and take them by surprise, even to the point of your own discomfort and sacrifice.

Fight on Your Terms

Another step to achieving success is to fight on your terms. There is no success without struggle, but if you are the one who determines when and where the struggle takes place, it will always be to your advantage. You never want to be reactionary; you always want to be proactive. Reaction, while sometimes unavoidable, means someone else is dictating your behavior. If you are proactive, you are the one who is determining what happens next. The best way to remain proactive is to always be aware of the power you possess or have access to, and do not be afraid to use it.

Consider for a moment the power of the individual citizen of the United States. Each has the right to vote. That vote has the power to send people to, or remove them from, the office where policies and decisions regarding our nation are made. The mind-set of most Americans is that their vote only counts on Election Day, but the truth is it counts every day. It is your voice; it is why your elected official will take your phone call. Based on his or her behavior, if your elected official ignores you, you may indeed begin to persuade others to vote that official out of office. In effect, you are the official's *boss*; that person is not your dictator. You possess the power; don't be afraid to use it. For far too long the citizenship of the United States has been duped into believing that we are forced to live with the appointed government. The frightening fact is that if we do not begin to use our freedom to defend our freedom, we will lose our freedom, and the perception that our appointed government has become our dictator rather than one that is subject to our election decisions *will become reality*.

Possess What Rightfully Belongs to You

The final rule of engagement is to refuse to allow anyone to possess what belongs to you. There are a great number of people in the world today who have given up on the dreams and aspirations they once had. There was a point in time when a fire burned within them that sparked fresh ideas and fueled a desire that could have shaped destiny, but that's all over now. Why? Because somewhere along the way they lost a battle, and in losing the battle, they quit. They failed to learn the lesson of failure—get up and fight on. These are the authors who refuse to write the books because they are afraid they won't be published. They are the singers who are silent because, as much as they wish to sing, the enemy of fear has them locked in a quiet penitentiary. It is the artist whose masterpiece will never be seen, the poet whose pen will never touch paper, the dreamer who has allowed the enemy of failure to dictate his reality, and the leader who has allowed the enemy of rejection to squander his gift. For each of them there is a great future to possess if they will simply have the courage to take the next step. Remember, if you don't do it, someone else will, and when they do, they may indeed possess what was set aside and intended for you.

Just because you do not achieve what you set out to accomplish the first time doesn't mean you have failed. Only when you cease to try have you failed. As long as there is breath in your lungs and the sun shining in the sky, don't you dare give up; live to fight another day. "Some days you'll get the bear; some days the bear gets you." No matter what, *don't quit.*

Step 1.6: Lessons I've Learned From Loss

- I cannot fail as long as I refuse to quit.

- Paying attention truly pays off.

- My enemies are real, but I can defeat them with the right amount of courage, knowledge, and determination to try.

Questions to Consider

1. What have I given up on that I truly need to try again?

_____

_____

2. What powers do I possess that I can use to turn things around?

_____

_____

3. What is the number one enemy that I need to confront and destroy (fear, rejection, doubt, bitterness, insecurity)?

_____

_____

Step 1.7

BE PATIENT...IT COMES IN STAGES

I AM ENDING THIS first section on personal responsibility with this final lesson: be patient. I have found that the hardest part about patience is the waiting! By my own inherited nature I am not a patient person, but throughout my life I've learned that revolutionary change is, in fact, an *evolutionary process*. In the introduction of this section I mentioned two pivotal dates: 1981, the year of the first Night to Honor Israel, and 2006, the year of the first Christians United for Israel Summit in Washington DC. The twenty-five years that separate these two major moments in time represent two and half decades of an evolving effort to a cause that in the last five years has quickly revolutionized the voice of Christianity in the halls of Congress on matters related to Israel and the Jewish people. I am reiterating all of this to say if you want to be an *overnight success*, you'll probably have to work hard and wait twenty-five years, but when patience pays off—it's worth it!

No matter what you want to change in your life physically, financially, spiritually, and emotionally, you should never expect to arrive where you want to go overnight. Remember, life is a series of commencements and completions, followed by another commencement. As soon as you achieve success in one area, a new struggle begins, and, thankfully, a new opportunity to be successful arises. The best news of all is that success is measured by the end result—not your current status.

I really like Joseph. He, by far, demonstrates the power and resolve needed to turn things around and revolutionize the world. Had Joseph ever considered himself a shepherd like his brothers, he would have settled for the status quo, taken off his coat, and watched over the flock with the rest of them. If he had not declared his own personal war on *average*, he would never have been thrown in the pit or sold into slavery or had the opportunity to distinguish himself in Potiphar's house. While in prison, if he had not invested himself in others, he would never have interpreted the dream that eventually made him known to Pharaoh. Had Joseph not lived a submitted life to his God, his bitterness would have destroyed his potential, and he would not have achieved his destiny as second only to Pharaoh in Egypt. If he didn't live upon principle, but rather on passion, Joseph would have had killed his brothers when they stood before him years later. Instead, on that day Joseph was able to be thankful because he had been prepared for his tomorrows and could speak these words, "You meant evil against me; but God meant it for good" (Genesis 50:20).

Joseph applied every step at the right time and in the right way, and it made his dream a reality. Before this can happen in your life, you need to remember that it is not your *current status* that matters; it is your *end result.* You may be scrubbing someone else's floor today, but if you take the right steps, you can be on the throne tomorrow. Too many people quit because of where they are rather than staying focused on where they are going. Don't get distracted by your circumstance; keep reaching for your destiny.

One of the ways to stay encouraged is to continually monitor your progress. I recommend that you gather data daily, measure progress monthly, and celebrate yearly. There are a lot of people who can get too focused on the task at hand and forget to take time to enjoy the moment. Celebrations are ordained of God, and I can think of nothing greater to celebrate than His faithfulness and blessings. Collecting data daily will help you to know if the plan you have made is working and will enable you to make adjustments where needed in order to stay on the path of success. Taking the time to compile the data on a regular basis will help you to determine if you need to do anything further to help in your progress, or if you are doing all that you can at the present moment. This kind of system, no matter where it is applied, will enable you to enjoy the things that are working, and it will help to prevent burnout and frustration.

Keep this in mind: You make the difference by taking one step at a time. Faithfully taking the next step will enable you to determine how fast and how far you can go. It's like the guy who drives eighty miles per hour for one hour versus the guy who only drives forty miles per hour for the same length of time. Taking the proper step at the proper time accelerates your rate of speed.

The contrary is also true. Taking the wrong step can send you all the way back to the beginning, hindering your progress and keeping you from making the turnaround that you are looking for.

Once you know what you are supposed to do, there is simply no time to waste. The process of making a long-lasting and successful change is indeed fragile enough—without neglect and procrastination adding to the problem. The moment you have made up your mind that your world needs to turn around and you need a revolution, get started—and don't look back! Never doubt that you have what it takes. Always look for a way to inspire others to believe in your cause. If you do, the changes you can bring to the world will indeed send shock waves and astound you.

Section 1 Review: Seven Lessons of Personal Responsibility

1.1 Respond based on principle.

1.2 Responsible people are submitted people.

1.3 Personally declare war on the status quo.

1.4 Be thankful for today and prepared for tomorrow.

1.5 Generously invest in others.

1.6 When you lose a battle, don't lose the war.

1.7 Be patient—it comes in stages.

Question to Consider

1. Which of these steps do I need to apply to my life today?

_____

_____

_____

Section Two

SOCIAL RESPONSE-ABILITY

Seven Lessons That Will Change the World Around You

I N 1978 MY father formed Global Evangelism, Inc. You must realize that upon its founding, it wasn't all that *global*. As a matter of fact, there were few outside the membership of Cornerstone Church who knew it even existed. Its mission statement was to "Preach All the Gospel to All the World," and that still holds true today. More than thirty-two years later, there isn't a place on the planet where Pastor Hagee isn't recognized as a preacher of the gospel. I remember well the first stages of the television ministry—and the sacrificial giving from the few hundred church members who believed the idea that *Global Evangelism* was possible from their meager campus in San Antonio.

I remember some of the first television viewers to call the church receptionist and ask how they could purchase a cassette tape or make a donation to help the ministry to continue to grow. I remember our very first fund-raising goal and how we cried tears of joy when we exceeded it. In my lifetime I've seen Global Evangelism go from a vision cast by an independent pastor with the support of a few members to an international ministry impacting the lives of millions every day. From this experience I've learned seven lessons that will change the world around you.

I've met so many individuals who have a great idea, vision, or concept that can truly be life changing for the world around them, but too often it seems they are afraid to share it, pursue it, or believe it can work.

The purpose of section 2 is to take your idea from a concept to a movement others can join, and from a movement to a force, and from a force to a fact.

I am an avid history buff; consider the concept of freedom that the Founding Fathers of this nation first had the courage to share with each other. Soon it became a movement, then a force, and finally a fact. It not only changed their reality, but it also improved the quality of life for generations to come. None of us witnessed the birth of this nation following the American Revolution, but we certainly have witnessed the impact of a different type of social revolution that has had as much of an impact as the revolution of the 1770s. Let me set the scene.

Imagine, if you will, the inauguration ceremony of the first president of the United States. Veterans who have sacrificed so very much to see this dream become a reality surround the stage. There is no "Star-Spangled Banner" to be played, because it has not been written yet. There is only the promise of freedom today and the hope of a better tomorrow. General George Washington lays his hand upon a book that he reads every morning and every night, one that in his memoirs he would identify as the book that gave him the strength he needed every day of his life. He takes the oath of office to be a leader who will represent, defend, and serve the people of this new nation.

Imagine, if you will, that he walked to the podium and began to give the first inaugural address—one that would serve as the template for all that followed—and do so by describing the America of today. That speech would be much different from the one of measured wisdom that we read in history books and biographies. In his speech today he would be addressing a much different America. It would be an America where those who sought religious freedom had the threat of lawsuits and legal action held like swords against their throats. That speech would describe a society that murders forty-three million plus children, in some cases with dollars collected by the federal government from taxpayers. That speech would describe a culture willing to defend destructive material and content such as pornography and make it available at public libraries to be viewed by anyone who chooses, regardless of their age.

What if General George Washington, considered by a vast majority of Americans as the *father of our nation*, described an America where there would be an all-out social offensive set against faith, family, and the social well-being of our children's futures? Where businessmen, laymen, and wage earners would be taxed severely to support those who can work but won't? The second American Revolution would have started that very day! However, the world described in this hypothetical speech is closer to our reality than the one Washington fought and sacrificed to create and defend.

How did it happen? It began with a social revolution led by groups called the American Civil Liberties Union (ACLU). It has been planned and carried out for more than eighty years. At first it took the established leadership by surprise because many considered it far too radical to ever take root. Then it became a movement, then a force, and now it is an all-out cultural revolution—a fact; one that must be addressed and one from which we truly need a change.

There is another social revolution that is worth mentioning. It is one that was planned and executed centuries ago. It has impacted not only this nation but also the nations of the world, and it has changed lives, enabled and empowered the weak and hopeless, and brought peace to the distraught and relief to the oppressed. This revolution began when heaven invaded the earth and the Son of God was born.

He motivated and inspired a handful of followers by looking them in the eye and saying, "Follow Me." He changed thousands of lives with the miracles He performed. He shattered the traditional mindset that said the common man was powerless to change his life and established a revolution that, by the very account of those who have seen it, "turned the world upside down" (Acts 17:6).

You see, social revolution is a powerful force for good *or* evil and is dependent upon who has the courage to use it. In the following pages I want to share seven lessons that will change the world around you and create a culture of responsibility that can turn a generation.

Step 2.1

PUT THINGS BACK IN PLACE

I AM, BY NO means, a technical person. For the longest time I heard people refer to the Nintendo Wii game system and thought when they said, "I have a Wii," that they needed directions to the restroom. Like it or not, technology is a major factor in our everyday life and something we have to at least learn to cope with. Here at Cornerstone, we, like many others, have individuals on staff whose primary and singular focus is computer maintenance and technology. For them I am a bit of a problem child, because while they can freely *talk to their computers*, I am either silent or yelling at mine. When the time comes for their intervention and mediation to reconcile my PC differences, I notice that they always begin with what they call a *reboot*. No matter how jammed up I may have gotten things, and regardless of all the mixed signals I have sent, with the simple turning off and restarting of the machine, it seems that all is forgiven and forgotten, and we can begin again. A reboot doesn't resolve everything, but it does cover a multitude of transgressions.

There are times in life when we need a *reboot*—a moment when we can stop, regroup, and start over. It may not be a miracle cure, but in many cases a simple reboot would help. If society is going to change, I recommend we start with a reboot. Take a moment and look back at where we began, and consider what is out of place that needs to be addressed, so that real progress and real change can be made.

As a child, when I was corrected, as soon as discipline had been administered, I continued in relationship with my parents as if the misbehavior had never occurred. I was held accountable, but following the chastening there was no change in the relationship I had with my parents. I was still their son; they still loved me with every fiber of their beings. They just had to take a moment and reboot my mental computer back to their original settings. As soon as things were put back in place, we carried on as normal. I think doing the same in families today would do our society a lot of good.

No matter what culture you study, at its center you will discover faith and religion. When we consider how to start over and reboot society, the church must be the place where the correction begins. There are a great number of people who would like to pretend that the church has nothing to do with society, but the truth is they are inseparable. It's a cyclical process. The people in the world make up the congregation. The mind-set of the home is the one the families bring to the sanctuary. The decisions made in the sanctuary are the behaviors that impact society. The attitude of society is what shapes the future and determines the quality of life for tomorrow. The quality of life is what sets the attitude and mind-set of the home, which is brought to the worship service on Sunday. If the world is going to change, the church—the center of faith, worship, and education—has to get back in its proper place. We need a reboot.

The sanctuary has become silent concerning society and has forgotten how to fight for what is just and right. We have taken the mindset that the house of God is a life raft for those who are looking for relief from a sinking ship, and we hope the raft will stay afloat until help arrives. That is a far cry from the position of the church when it was begun.

In the Book of Acts we find a church that was operating in a hostile political and cultural environment. Political and religious leaders were doing everything within their power to hinder the newly birthed church. Christians were thrown into jail for preaching and tortured in an attempt to force them to deny their faith. In some cases the leaders of congregations were killed in order for political and religious leaders to obtain public approval. How did that first church respond? It fought back. Not by picking up swords and shedding blood in the street, but by declaring the message all the more boldly. By feeding the hungry, praying over and administering health and wellness to the sick, educating and bringing equality to the oppressed, and by providing for the poor.

These powerful actions created a movement and force that no dictator could control and no enemy could destroy. The question is, if it worked in the first century, why not now? Yet today's church is refusing to take responsibility for who we are and what we are to provide to society. In many cases we are considered to be a Far Right group that likes to yell as much about our cause as the Far Left does about theirs. We sound good on Sunday, but we do very little come Monday. If we are going to create a social revolution for the good, then this behavior has to stop. The church must get back in the fight and take up arms against the issues that are the most pressing to the welfare of men. If we do, the other things that we are so embattled over will, in many cases, resolve themselves as they fade from center stage, and what is truly important becomes our focus again.

The church must fight on four fronts in order to change the world. We must take an offensive against hunger, sickness, ignorance, and poverty. When the church begins to provide answers to these challenges, society will cease to look to the government that craves control and power in exchange for its services and get back to being what we are supposed to be—a nation of the people, by the people, and for the people.

Consider hunger. In the first century the church was described as sharing all things and having all things in common. They went from house to house breaking bread, eating their food with gladness, praising God and having favor with all the people. (See Acts 2.) Historians have established that the first-century church in Jerusalem numbered about sixty thousand adherents. That's more than a few mouths to feed! Acts 6:1 states, "When the number of the disciples was multiplying..." It's a fact that to multiply you at least double in number. Consider that on the Day of Pentecost three thousand people were added to the one hundred twenty in the Upper Room, and from that time forward "the Lord added to the church daily" (Acts 2:47).

It isn't difficult to establish that before long the church of Acts was a much larger crowd than the average home Bible study of today.

So how did they do it? How did they feed all of those people? The answer is given in one word: *willingly.* They willingly gave, they willingly shared, and they willingly took care of one another. No one forced them to do it; they wanted to do it. The Bible describes their attitude as one of "gladness and simplicity of heart" (Acts 2:46). No one can do something they are being forced to do *with gladness.* The food needs of the first-century Christians were met not by a federal government's food stamp program collected in the form of taxes from those who were willing to work in order to feed those who refuse to work. The first-century Christians' needs were met by fellow believers. This fact developed deep loyalty and admiration between the members and empowered them to stick together in the midst of the most difficult and trying times.

Earlier I mentioned those who through their support helped make Global Evangelism a reality. How did they do it? Willingly! They were glad to be a part of something they felt had the potential to change the world through the preaching of the Word.

The reason I believe we need a reboot in this generation is because *willingness* is one of the last words I would use to describe our overall outlook on life. We are stubborn, and very seldom are we willingly involved in anything that will not personally benefit us, much less bless others. When you talk about the basic functions of the first-century church that worked so very well, people will rebut with, "It won't work!" Sure it will; you just have to be willing to let it work.

We, the modern church, have just become accustomed to letting the government do it, and then we complain about the poor job they are doing. My grandmother had a rule in her house that I think should be etched on the doorposts of every church in America. "Do not complain about what you are willing to allow." Message: If you don't like it, change it! If you want to change the way the needs of the hungry are met in your city, community, or church, then start feeding them!

You may not be able to feed them all, but remember, if you can inspire and motivate people to join in your cause, you can start a movement that becomes a force, creating a revolution that becomes a fact.

What if every member of your church bought one additional food item every time he or she went to the grocery store for the purpose of donating the item for a meal that would be hosted on a regular basis at your church? You wouldn't have to buy $100 worth of tenderloins but something that could be added to the whole and used to meet the needs of those in the community area. Volunteers could prepare the food, and the hungry would be brought in so they could eat with those who had provided and prepared the meal. The program wouldn't be identical from church to church, but at least the church would be providing a solution to a real world issue, and that one step can revolutionize society.

We should declare war on sickness. Healing and well-being have always been a major issue of concern in the world. Today, one of the most hotly contested topics of the nation is health care. We can sit back and join the parade of political personalities ranting about how wrong the other side is, or we can revolutionize the world by declaring war on sickness.

Have you ever looked at the number of hospitals that have the name of a religious organization in their titles? All over the country you see Baptist hospitals, Methodist hospitals, Catholic hospitals, and the list goes on. This is not a matter of coincidence; it demonstrates that when these particular organizations began, they were faith-based and sponsored by the church. Their intention was to administer healing to the sick and prevent diseases. In the first century, one of the major contributing factors to the success of the church and its influence in society was the ability to bring healing.

You may say, "Well, that was divine healing." Indeed it was, but I do not consider the healing methods of modern science to be void of God's intervention but rather the extension of the same. James 1:17 says, "Every good gift and every perfect gift is from above."

In October 2008 my father and my mother-in-law underwent open-heart surgeries, which saved their lives. Neither would be here today without those surgeries. Since 2006 I have had three family members need surgery to cut cancer out of their bodies. In each case the individual was sedated prior to surgery as cancer patients—and woke up in recovery cancer free. These were not the works of men void of God's touch; they were moments where God divinely intervened to restore the health of people I dearly love.

It is, and always has been, God's desire to heal. He promised this fact to the nation of Israel the moment He brought them out of captivity in Egypt: "For I am the LORD who heals you" (Exodus 15:26). He has not changed. Healing has always been at the forefront of the work of the Lord and should be in the heart of His people on Earth today. Think of how many faith-based organizations travel to the farthest outreaches of the world to participate in medical missions. They give preventive and basic care to those who otherwise wouldn't be able to receive it. They do it in the name of the Lord, and through their kindness they demonstrate His love to those who are searching for answers.

Why not home-based medical missions? What sense does it make to go to the most remote jungle with a service that, in turn, we are unwilling to provide across the street or on the other side of town? Think of what a church could do if it would pool its resources together to have a medical mission truck. It could provide very basic and much-needed services to those who have a difficult time obtaining them right here at home—things like a simple eye exam, blood sugar screening, blood pressure readings, or free dental cleaning, all of which are easily administered and are able to make a tremendous difference in a person's overall health and well-being.

You might say, "Well, they really don't need the church to do that, because the government already does." That's the problem! The church has allowed the government to take its place in providing the basic needs to our fellow men in society. By doing so, rather than having a system that is founded on the principles of faith and family, we have one that is void of reverence for God and in many cases mocks and even denies Him. It's time to put things back in place and reboot a system that's not working.

What do you think would happen in your city if your church had a medical mission truck with a sonogram machine? What if a young lady in an inner-city neighborhood brings her elderly relative to the truck to have vital readings taken and in passing tells one of the volunteers on the team that she thinks she might be about two months pregnant? A quick sonogram would reveal if she's right, and rather than going to the nearest government-funded clinic where she is not given the opportunity to see the growing child inside her or to even hear the heartbeat but would be strongly advised to have an abortion, she is in a truck where she can see for herself the miracle of life.

Not all of her hard questions would be answered, and certainly she would need additional support to help with the challenge of being a single mom, but at least a life would be saved rather than thrown away in the senseless act of abortion. Besides, I would be willing to bet that the church that provides this kind of medical service would also be able to provide food to the mother and child if she required it and maybe even assist her in finding a family to adopt the child if that were her choice. You may say, "I just don't think those kinds of things happen." I promise you—they will not if you don't try.

What about education? What can the church do about that? The battlefield of the mind is the most crucial area of all when determining the quality of life for the future of the nation. He who sits in front of the classroom is like a sculptor who is chiseling out what will be tomorrow's monument. We can revolutionize the world through the classroom.

As in health care, there was a time when the church was at the center of education. Long before there were state-supported colleges and universities, the church was the resource of education for society. The best part about this kind of education is that the fear of God was at the center of it. We read in Psalm 111:10, "The fear of the LORD is the beginning of wisdom." Why is it, then, that so many so-called *campuses of higher learning* seem to have lost their minds? It is because they have ceased to fear the Lord. They may believe they are in pursuit of knowledge, but everything they find will be devoid of any wisdom. What is the solution? The church needs to declare war on ignorance and misinformation and get back in the fight of education.

Not every church can afford a school, and not every family can afford private education, but consider some of these options. A volunteer in the congregation could teach a free GED program for those in your city who would like to earn their diplomas. While the class would cover all that is required on the exam concerning reading, writing, and arithmetic, there would be a reverence and respect for God at the center of the course. By empowering someone to better his or her life through this type of setting, you can truly turn around that person's life and the life of that family for generations.

What would happen in any given city if a number of churches were willing to overcome their own pride and egos and come together to create a consolidated Christian school? Each participant could be confident that the curriculum would not only prepare the children for success in life, but it would also build upon an unshakable foundation of faith, which they all share. However, rather than willingly admit Christ-centered education is in our best interest, we stubbornly argue doctrinal differences.

Then consider what would happen if local businesses started relationships with local Christian schools in order to find deserving children in their community whose educations they would be willing to sponsor in return for those children coming to work for their companies one day, thereby securing the businesses needs for qualified and ethical work forces. The possibilities are truly endless—if you are willing to sit down and consider them.

The final battlefront that the church must engage in is poverty. Through programs like the ones listed above, many of the needs created by poverty can be met, and many of the scenarios that cause poverty can be prevented. But what would happen if the church went beyond that and created a presence in the community through its buying power that couldn't be denied? What if your church went to a local grocery store and negotiated terms with the store that would allow every member of the congregation to shop at this store at a discounted rate? The grocer could secure future income and customer loyalty and make more money through the number of clients he would gain as opposed to the few additional pennies of profit he would be willing to give back in trade. The same arrangements could be made with banks and other essential businesses in the community. This would certainly establish the church as much more than a place where one stops by for an hour and half on Sunday for *spiritual hors d'oeuvres*.

These types of programs are exactly what society is in need of and what we as a church should be providing. You may have a long list of reasons why they might not work, but the truth is there are no laws against doing good deeds, and no one can stop you from making a difference in the lives of others. You just need to mentally reboot your system into believing it's possible. You can be responsible for a social revolution that will turn your city, your county, your state, your nation, and your world around. We must each do our individual and collective parts and, in doing so, become a force that changes the lives of millions from the bottom up, one day at a time.

Step 2.1: Putting Things Back in Place

- Social revolution happens from the bottom up.

- I cannot complain about what I am willing to allow.

- I cannot change what I will not confront; the time has come for the confrontation to begin.

Questions to Consider

1. What are the names of three people I know whom I can inspire to help me start a social movement?

    _____

    _____

2. What area of need in the lives of others can I help change right now?

    _____

    _____

3. What mind-set and attitudes do I need to change in order to go from being a part of the problem to creating a solution?

    _____

    _____

Step 2.2

DON'T STOP WORKING

I COME FROM A long line of extremely hardworking people. My father's mother ran her own business until she was in her mid-eighties. My father got a job as a birthday present when he turned eight. The summer I turned thirteen I went to work unloading eighteen-wheelers filled with produce on the docks of my Grandpa Castro's produce terminal. Work started at 3:00 a.m. and ended when you were done. Needless to say, a few South Texas summer days unloading fruit and vegetable trucks gives you real appreciation for what makes the world go round—*work*!

If you want to make a real difference, you are going to have to work and work hard. There are no set hours; begin early and stop when you're done. Then go to bed satisfied that you did all you could do, and look forward to trying again in the morning. I know from observation and experience that this kind of enthusiasm for work is contagious, and when others join your cause, a movement will soon follow. When others are willing to work alongside you, you are taking advantage of the power of agreement.

Being in agreement means that two entities that are not alike have come together for a common cause. People in our society throw around loosely the word *agreement* or *unity*, to the point that it loses meaning. Unity is truly a powerful element in life and in relationships. To help you regain its meaning, let me give you an example from the Hagee house.

Those who have spent time with my parents know firsthand what unity can accomplish. As individuals, they are two totally different people. My dad has a very type A personality—turbo charge, full speed ahead; if you cannot jump over it, lower your head and blast through it. My mother's gift, on the other hand, is hospitality. She can make the most frigid person warm up and feel welcome. She takes the time to consider the individual likes and dislikes of all and in every way possible goes above and beyond to make sure everyone is happy and content. My mother's motto is, "May I get you anything else?" My father's creed is, "If you can't hack it, get your jacket."

How do these two things work together? In unity! They may be very different, but they come into agreement about what they want to accomplish and become united in the effort to get it done. Dad inspires, motivates, and leads the masses. Mom makes sure they enjoy the ride. One does not accomplish near as much without the other, and both require a great deal of work and dedication to be successful. If my parents didn't have agreement in marriage, the home would have become a war zone.

The same is true in every other relationship. Without agreement in music, the band that was supposed to play in one accord has the opposite effect, which is discord. You do not have to be exactly alike in order to be unified, but you must have agreement with one another in spite of your differences; otherwise there will be no harmony. I have sung with my family since I was a child. When we were young, my father taught us how to sing in harmony. Each of us had a totally different note that we were to sing, but when all the notes were sung simultaneously, they created a common and pleasant sound that was much fuller and sweeter together than at any point alone.

If we are going to make a difference in this generation, if we are going to move forward with the right response, we must work in harmony with one another. We do not have to lose our individual identity, but we do have to work together. When we do, we are stronger and happier than we would ever be alone.

Look at the family in your home and apply this truth for a moment. My wife and I are not at all the same. We approach issues with different perspectives, and our daily responsibilities are totally different. In our situation we both work: I work outside the home, and her job is inside. Mine is the business and work of the ministry and the church as well as our private family affairs. Hers is raising our children. You may think, "Well, that's not work," but the only reason you would say it is because you have never tried it. Believe me, three children under the age of five is work every day all day. As a matter of fact, when I get home from the office, I clock in on my second shift responsibilities, because until the kids go to sleep, a father's active involvement is absolutely required. Then, as if that were not enough, once they're in bed, you have to pick up the pieces of evidence that they left behind in the crime scene of the living room and make all of the necessary arrangements for the fun to begin again the very next day.

Should either my wife or I decide to stop working in agreement with each other, the business of our family would cease to function properly. We are not at all alike, but we each respect and assist each other in what we are trying to do. It's the harmony in the home that makes life sweet and empowers a man and his family to make their mark on the world.

If anything is going to work appropriately in your life, agreement is an absolute essential. No one was ever intended to live life alone. From the very beginning God established, "It is not good that man should be alone" (Genesis 2:18). As a matter of fact, you could go so far as to say that out of all of the things that the Lord created, *man* was the only thing that He went back and made an adjustment on. He decided that a man wasn't complete without a woman. If your life is going to be all that it was intended to be, find the one God created for you, and learn to live in harmony with that person.

Everything is made better with harmony—not just marriages, but churches, cities, and entire societies. How much destruction have you seen as the result of stubborn attitudes that created a dividing line in a team or partnership? One or both parties would rather live in isolation with an attitude of *at least I'm right* than strive for agreement. What if each person offered his or her unique abilities to the entire team in order to see everyone succeed? This is possible if all the team members are willing to agree, unify, and fill the missing ingredient in the team with their talents.

It is a fact that it's not always possible to work together, because there are indeed things that each of us must accomplish alone. However, make sure that your individual efforts are still striving for the success of others in an attempt to reach a collective goal as opposed to fulfilling self-motivated interests. When you do work alone, make sure that the work you are doing is for your family, your church, and your team. Work together when you can, work alone when you must, but don't stop working!

When you have to fly solo, it doesn't necessarily mean that you are taking the world on alone. It may mean that it is your time to grow and develop the necessary skills in your life that will ultimately be of benefit to others later. However, if that is not the reason for your isolation, then it is void of purpose.

When I went away to the university, unlike many of my friends with whom I graduated from high school, I went alone. I'll be the first to tell you that I had no clue how that experience was going to impact me. All of my life I had been surrounded by friends and family and closely connected to a group of peers and people throughout the church. When I landed in Tulsa, eight hundred plus miles away, I thought I had been placed in solitary confinement. However, after enduring that season of my life, I had developed a much clearer picture of who I really was. Because I had been removed from what I considered to be comfortable and familiar, I saw things in me that in any other environment would not have been revealed. The personal lessons I learned in college enabled me to come home to the place I left behind as a child and minister as a man.

You may be wondering, "Why do I feel like I am going through a world where I have been left alone and no one sees me?" If that is the case, then take a moment and ask yourself why you feel isolated. If it is by choice, then decide to reconcile the relationships that you walked away from and begin living in harmony and agreement yet again. If, on the other hand, you are isolated through no choice of your own but due to circumstances, then think about what it is you are there to learn, and master it so you can be a resource and a blessing to others later on. Being able to understand this period of isolation is only for a season to provide you with a greater purpose in your future that will give you the strength to get through another day.

Once the season of solitude is over, you'll see that the change in you will revolutionize the team you are a part of and that the harmony you create working in agreement with others is the exact kind of music the world longs to hear.

Step 2.2: Don't Stop Working

- Unity does not mean losing your identity; it simply means working with others in agreement.

- There are certain things you must do on your own, but they will be a blessing for the greater good in the future.

- We are not intended to face life alone; we are relational beings.

Questions to Consider

1. In what ways have I isolated myself from others whom I can be of help to?

_____

_____

2. Do I truly take the time to appreciate the difference that people make in my life? Can I identify the difference that I make in theirs?

_____

_____

3. Whom can I encourage by coming into agreement with today?

_____

_____

Step 2.3

FIXING THE FOUNDATION

THE AREA OF Texas where I live is covered in limestone. As a matter of fact, if you want to dig a hole, forget about using a shovel and just get a jackhammer. From time to time the limestone underneath the ground shifts a little here and there and can create problems in the foundations of the homes that are built above. Most of the time these foundational issues are first seen in the doors of the home, which will no longer shut, and rather than fit in the frame, they seem to be out of alignment. Then there are the more noticeable hairline cracks in the wall. At first you might think that a little paint and Spackle will cover it up—after all, out of sight is out of mind—but if the issue is a foundational one, sooner later the crack will reappear. Even worse than cracks in the walls are broken pipes in the foundation, which can cause severe damage. Understand that if the problem is critical enough—and ignored long enough—you may lose your structure altogether. Here's the point: if you have a foundational problem, there's no point in camouflaging it; you have to fix it, and the sooner, the better.

For the purpose of this section, the structure we are talking about is the church. But there are a lot of foundational issues in other areas of life that are as equally important to address when they arise. The quality of your foundation will determine your ability to succeed and endure. No matter what part of your life is affected—marital, personal, financial, spiritual—if the foundation is faulty, nothing else will be right. One of the verses we memorized in our home growing up was, "If the foundations are destroyed, what can the righteous do?" (Psalm 11:3).

The problem with our society is that the foundation is in great need of repair. The church should be the foundation of our culture. The reason the church is struggling to take its proper place in this culture is because the people in the church have forgotten their role within its structure. We, the church, are a body created to function under the authority of our head, who is Jesus Christ. No one is able to physically function if it is disconnected from the head. Nor can a body that is always at war with itself properly function. Unfortunately, there are a great number of churches around the country and the world where both of these problems exist. Until they are addressed, making a difference in the world will be just a dream or a fairy tale.

Where do we begin addressing the problem? My first recommendation is that we get back to the basics. Churches today have so many differing focuses that we need an entire study devoted to *Churchology* in order to understand them all. There are churches based on environment and atmosphere. There is the relaxed church, the formal church, the casual and contemporary church, the traditional church, the outdoor church, the cowboy church, the inner-city and urban church, the cultural church or multicultural church, the soft church and the ultrahardcore church, the political church, and the *come as you are* church. They're all out there and available for your choosing, taste, and preference if you like, but no matter what you call it, there are a few things that must be a part of each and every church before you can call them a church.

First and foremost is *the Word of God*. Without the Word, a church is nothing more than a Sunday social club, and its doors should be closed. It is the Word that changes the lives of those who come to worship on Sunday, whether in sermon or song. It is the Word that provides the answers to life's most difficult questions and provides the navigational beacons for the path that lies ahead. It is the Word that draws men to salvation, which overcomes doubt and fear, conquers sickness, cures disease, and promises eternity in heaven. No matter the venue where you choose to worship on Sunday, if you go and do not hear the Word, then you have wasted your time and certainly have not been to church.

On the other hand, if you are a person who is born of the Word, then anywhere you find the Word being preached and taught, you should feel at home. I think the church has gotten to the point where personal preferences have become a major hindrance. Even if someone is preaching the same truth we believe in, but just not doing it as we think they should, we disqualify them from our fellowship. We have gotten way too focused on the *method* and have totally lost sight of the *message*. I don't care if you are the kind of person who likes attending church in an outdoor arena or a rural area surrounded by God's creation. The Word that is preached there should be the same as the Word preached in a church in the innermost part of the biggest city, and you should feel comfortable in both places. What you are looking for at church should not have as much to do with environment as it does with content, and the content you seek is the Word.

The church should be a place where you feel the presence of the Lord. Remember that the church house is *His* house, and if you can't feel Him when you come through the doors, something is wrong. In Luke 4:18 Jesus stood up in the synagogue and read from the Book of Isaiah, saying, "The Spirit of the Lord is upon Me, because He has anointed Me to preach the gospel to the poor..." Notice that the Word and the Spirit always seem to go together. Where you find one, you'll find the other, and where the two are at work, you will see results.

The final thing that should be in every church is results. You cannot claim to represent a God who has promised in His Word to take you from glory to glory and be the same all the time. You should be growing, winning the lost, changing lives, and seeing people who were searching for direction and a sense of purpose become those who are living a life of promise. If you don't think so, look what Christ said in the rest of Luke 4:18:

> He has sent Me to heal the brokenhearted,
> To proclaim liberty to the captives

And recovery of sight to the blind,
To set at liberty those who are oppressed.

Every one of those proclamations can be measured by results. If the church will be what it has been called to be, the results should revolutionize the lives of those who are willing to receive and cannot be denied by those who resist it.

Once the proper elements are in place in the church, the next step that must take place is for the people of the church to become who they were called to be. We are those who have been set apart. We are described as a "peculiar people" (1 Peter 2:9, KJV). We are special—not that we are any better than anyone else, but we have been blessed by the excellent greatness of God, and therefore His excellence should be the difference in our lives. The Bible is a book of excellence; therefore the people of the Bible should be people of excellence.

You should possess excellence of mind; your thought life should be set on the things that are good, true, noble, just, and of good report (Philippians 4:8).

You should be excellent in body; your physical body is a gift created for you by God, and to do anything to intentionally destroy it is to take for granted the gift He gave.

You should be excellent in spirit. Peace of mind, joy in your heart, and confidence in who you are and what God has done for you should be the bedrock of your character. This is why the church is "in the world" but "not of the world" (John 17:11, 14). Because these elements are in you, you have set yourself apart from society and, in doing so, have the ability to transform the culture for the glory of God.

The church should be the center of the society, not divorced from it. We should have a presence and a voice in every form of civil government from the school board to the city hall. We should have a very clear presence in the area of education. Too many Christians have bought into the misinformation that faith is not allowed in the public forum. That is not true; your faith may not be *welcomed*, but it is every bit as *allowed* as any other form of speech and expression. The question is, do you have enough confidence in yourself and the Word to be the kind of person who demands the attention of the audience rather than just getting lost in the crowd?

When I was in the third grade, our class was given the assignment to write an essay on Christmas traditions and celebrations in other countries. We were encouraged to pick a nation that represented our heritage, so I chose Mexico and wrote on the festival known as *Las Posadas*, the Spanish word for "the passing." Each of the elementary grades was given the same assignment, and the paper that was considered to be the best from each grade was to be read the week before Christmas break. Out of all of the third grade classes at the school, my paper was nominated by my teacher and chosen to be read by all of the other teachers there at the school.

I was ecstatic and went home to tell my parents the good news. The week before Christmas break came, and I was fully prepared to read my essay over the public address system before school began. However, just as the day ended, I was called to the principal's office because she needed to tell me something about my paper. You see, *Las Posadas* is a celebration where the children in the community would dress as Mary and Joseph and go from place to place in search of a place to have the Christ child. It is obviously a reenactment of the account given in the Book of Luke.

It was two words in my essay that created the problem. The principal informed me that because my paper contained the words *Christ child*, approval could not be given for it to be read over the loudspeaker. I would either have to change the essay or not be able to participate. So, being a normal third grader, I went home and told my dad what the principal had told me, only to return with him the next morning to wait for the principal to arrive so we could talk and come to a clearer understanding.

Every third grader is scared of their principal, but I'll never forget watching my father look her in the eyes and very clearly ask, "Where does it state in the school handbook or the state law or federal law that this paper is disqualified from being read because it mentions Christ?" She could offer no other response other than to claim that there was separation between church and state. Although she worked in education, she was ignorant of what the law really said about the matter. The next thing that my father said gave her a clear choice to make. She could either allow me to read the paper and take her chances with a rule she was uncertain as to whether it existed or not, or she could continue with her position and face a genuine lawsuit for discrimination.

Five minutes later, when the bell rang and the pledges were complete, I stood at the microphone and, with my father's hand holding the button that said "Talk," read every line of my essay loud and clear. That day I learned what defending the faith looked like. It's not a matter of taking everything you're told in stride; it is a matter of standing up for yourself and being who you were born to be—"the salt of the earth" and "the light of the world" (Matthew 5:13–14). When the church ceases to be afraid to be the church, then the gates of hell will not be able to prevail against us (Matthew 16:18).

We are a foundation of empowerment. It is on the foundation of the church that real problems will find solid answers and where destiny and divine appointment meet. If the church will get its foundation fixed, we will once again be the bedrock of society rather than its stepping-stone.

Step 2.3: Fixing the Foundation

- Every church should be filled with the Word of God, the Spirit of God, and the results of their divine work in the lives of men.

- No matter what your personal preference is, wherever you find the Word and the Spirit, you should feel right at home.

- Because the Bible is a book of excellence, the people who live by the Bible should be people of excellence.

Questions to Consider

1. Do I notice signs of foundational problems in my life, and if so, what am I going to do about it?

_____

_____

2. What positive results can I measure in my life and the lives of others by being a part of the church?

_____

_____

3. When is the last time I defended the faith and stood up in society for who I am in Christ?

_____

_____

Step 2.4

GET BACK TO THE BOOK

NEXT TIME YOU are in a convenience store, take a look at the measuring tape they have stuck to the door as you walk out. Its purpose is to give the clerk an idea of your height, should you become the perpetrator of a crime; the clerk also needs to give the police your description. Out of all of the convenience stores I have ever been in, no two measuring tapes are exactly alike. If I walk out of the one closest to my office, I measure in at about five feet ten inches—a few inches shorter than the medical chart at my doctor's office. If I fill up at the one by my house, then I am six foot four inches—if only for a moment, and only in my dreams.

The point is this: in order for an accurate measurement to be taken, there must be a consistent standard. Human nature is such that we like to compare ourselves against each other. Listen to young children when they first meet, and watch how they interact.

"How old are you?"

"I'm three!"

"Well, I'm four and going to be five next month, so I'm older!"

They will walk up to each other, stand on the tiptoes, and start trying to see who is taller. They will engage in acts of strength and show the other how high they can jump and what kind of somersault they can turn on the floor. They are always trying to measure up and determine who is the oldest, biggest, fastest, and smartest.

Many adults from all walks of life have a tendency to do the same. We consistently compare ourselves with one another and often find validation in the fact that we are doing better than the next guy. The problem with this standard is that it is ever changing, depending on the people by whom you are surrounded. If you are among an elite team of astrophysicists, you probably don't want to talk about science. If you are hanging out with preschoolers, you may indeed measure up as a genius. Only when there are proper standards established are you truly able to make an accurate assessment.

The church, society, and your personal life should only be measured by one standard, and that standard is the Word of God. It serves as His written and spoken standard of measurement. You, as an individual, are not to compare yourself with the person next to you. You are to compare yourself against the Word and see what it has to say about you. Your church is not to consider its success or failure based on what the church down the street is doing. Your church is to see what the Bible says about what it is to be doing and strive to accomplish that. Society may hold itself in comparison to civilizations of the past or present, but it must consider what standard the Word has said about life and then see that it follows those guidelines. Only when this takes place will we see a culture ready to respond to any challenge it may face.

The statement "All have sinned and fall short of the glory of God" (Romans 3:23) is not one of cruelty but of fact. The Bible is the recorded history of God's glory manifested in the lives of men throughout every generation and the revelation of what He will do in the future. When you see how marvelous He is, it doesn't take long to recognize that no one measures up. The only hope that we have is in God's amazing grace and mercy. He is willing to look upon us and determine that we are worthy to be called His own, not because we measure up to His standard but because He has loved us so deeply. He is willing to accept us on the basis of our acceptance of His Son. The power of those facts causes me to pause each time I think about it.

The only way to achieve change is to start living by a standard that creates change. The Bible is not a book that changes the lives of those who have learned to argue and debate it; it revolutionizes the lives of those who learn to live it. You cannot receive a blessing from something that you are always arguing with. Arguments are rooted in doubt, and the Word of God is lived out in faith. The sooner you stop debating the truth and start living the truth, the sooner you'll start making a difference.

There are two things that you must understand about the Bible that will change your life forever once you accept them and start living by them.

First, the Word is truth. It is not a book that is to be compared with other books to determine its value. It is the Book by which all other books are measured. If what is written in another book doesn't match up with the Bible, throw the other book away, because it is trash.

John wrote in his Gospel, "You shall know the truth, and the truth shall make you free" (John 8:32). Accepting and obeying this truth will set you free from poverty.

The Word promises that God will supply all of your needs (Philippians 4:19). Living in this truth will set you free from fear.

Psalm 27:1 states, "The LORD is my light and my salvation; whom shall I fear? The LORD is the strength of my life; of whom shall I be afraid?" The truth of God's Word will remove the burdens of sorrow, set you free from doubt, and overcome insecurity.

The truth of the Word of God can do all of that, and that is only the beginning.

Second, the Word of God is unchanging. Isaiah 40:8 states, "The grass withers, the flower fades, but the word of our God stands forever." I like to consider that verse in these terms: My situation may change, but my promises never do. Throughout my life I have faced a long list of ever-changing problems. Everyone has. No one is immune to the ever-changing circumstances of life. The blessing of living by the Word is that my problems may change, but my promise never does. It's always and forever the same, and I can count on it, no matter what.

Consider this. When I was a child, I was terrified of the dark. There, I said it! I had a good reason to be afraid of the dark. I loved to play outside as a kid, and my dad would come home from work and convert our backyard into an imaginary wonderland. We played in the World Series, ran for touchdowns in the Super Bowl, and fought in every world war. It was so much fun that I dreaded when the sun would go down and the fun ended. I always asked my dad if we could turn on the lights and play a little longer. His method of convincing me that was not a good idea was to say, "Son, you don't want to be outside when the sun goes down; that's when the bad people come out." Now I didn't know who the bad people were, but I knew if my dad didn't want to meet them, then neither did I.

This led me to looking at every shadow and listening to every sound as if they were going to eat me alive in the middle of the night. So I did what every believer should do; I made an appointment with my *pastor* to discuss the fear that I was experiencing as a result of what my *father* had told me.

My *pastor* taught me this declaration to make based on a promise in God's Word concerning my fear: "For God has not given us a spirit of fear, but of power and of love and of a sound mind" (2 Timothy 1:7). I quoted that verse many nights as a child until I fell asleep. I can gladly report to you that it has been awhile since I have had any issues with the dark. However, that doesn't mean that I don't still deal with fear from time to time. There is no shortage of fearful things in the world today that can take your breath away. Whether it is political, economic, global, concerning disease, safety, or security, just watch the evening news and take your pick. But while the problems that cause fear have changed—and will change—the promise has not. God has not given *me* a spirit of fear, but of power and of love and of a sound mind.

I don't have to worry or fret about the world that I am living in, because the God who lives in me is greater than the whole entire world. I'm not sure it can get much better than that. When you begin to put the Word back in the proper place at home and at church, then the church will start to get back in its proper place in the society.

Step 2.4: Get Back to the Book

- The only way to attain an accurate measurement is by having an immovable standard.

- The Word of God is the standard of truth.

- The problems may change, but the promise never does.

Questions to Consider

1. Do I compare my life in light of the standard of the Word or in light of those around me?

_____

_____

2. On what promise do I want to take a stand and start living by today?

_____

_____

Step 2.5

RECOGNIZING THE NATURAL HALF OF THE SUPERNATURAL

BY NOW IT should be pretty obvious that the *old-fashioned* tone of principles found in this book was molded and shaped by my father, best friend, and mentor. I believe that's the way God intended it to be and hopefully how it will be for my children someday.

To illustrate this next point, I want to tell you about a conversation I heard my dad having one day with one of the brightest minds and political figures of our day. They were discussing current events and how they saw a series of ongoing concerns playing out and affecting the world. While they agreed on the outcome, they had totally different responses. The gentleman, whom I do indeed respect, said, "Well, God is almighty, and if He wants to change it or stop it, He can do so by Himself." My father's response: "God is almighty, and while He doesn't need our help, He requires it; if He's going to do anything, He'll do it through us." I learned that day there is always a natural element to every supernatural work, and the natural half of the supernatural begins with you and me.

There are a number of people who take the approach that God is all-powerful and if He wants to do it, He can. But the fact remains that when God wants to do something, He involves man. His approach is to find someone who is willing to trust Him and then show that individual and the world what He can do through him or her. God's supernatural power needs a willing and able natural participant.

Consider the exodus of the children of Israel from Egypt. Could God have done that on His own? Certainly! But consider what He was able to do in and through the life of one man by appearing in a burning bush to a shepherd named Moses on the backside of the desert.

Without a doubt, God Almighty could have crushed Goliath in front of the entire Israelite army, but through the courage of a boy named David and one smooth stone, God was able not only to deliver a nation but also to establish a king and set up a royal dynasty.

God has always worked through men, and He wants to work through you if you will let Him. The first thing that He is looking for is *faithfulness*. The Word says, "'Well done, good and faithful servant; you have been faithful over a few things, I will make you ruler over many things. Enter into the joy of your lord.' ... To everyone who has, more will be given" (Matthew 25:23, 29). If we are faithful in the little things, we will be given greater things. I have heard a lot of people talk about the worldwide ministries that they want to start, but some of those same people are unwilling to teach a Sunday school class at their local churches. Most consider it to be beneath their level of talent and ability. Keep in mind that your talent and ability came from God, so every opportunity you have to give it back to Him is one more way you demonstrate your gratitude.

When my father began what is now a church of more than twenty thousand people over forty years ago in the city of San Antonio, he started with three families in a living room. There was no staff to manage, no budget to maintain, and no strategic plan to implement, but he was willing to do what God had called him to do and in the place he had been given the opportunity to do it. Now, forty years later, God's supernatural power has been poured out on the natural effort and faithfulness of my father's work and ministry, and the miraculous results are impacting the world today. From time to time I will listen to an audiotape from the early seventies when the church had just begun recording the services. It is amazing to me that while certain things have indeed changed, others absolutely have not. The commitment to the truth of the Word and the passion of the presentation were the same then as they are now. Those old tapes are a testament to faithfulness. Even though he was preaching to only hundreds, he prepared and presented as if it were tens of thousands.

Second, not only is God looking for you to be faithful, but He also wants you to *trust* Him. I have heard it said many times, "Do all that you can, and trust God for the rest." The important thing to remember about trust is that it.is a result of relationship. You cannot trust someone whom you do not know. You may take someone else's word of endorsement on his or her character, but until you get to know that person, real trust can't be developed. A lot of people today are trying to get by on someone else's endorsement of God's character. They have listened to preachers declare what God can do and heard others give testimony of His power, and they have thought, "Well, maybe He will do something like that for me someday."

The problem is that until you get to know God, you will not be able to truly put your trust in Him. We can see that in Jesus's earthly ministry; He seemed to hold the twelve disciples to a higher standard than others, based on their familiarity with who He was and what He could do. Look at the fourth chapter of Mark. The twelve are given instructions to sail a boat across the Sea of Galilee to the shore on the other side. In the midst of the journey, a great storm causes the disciples to fear for their lives. While they are struggling to keep the ship afloat, Christ is asleep in the back of the boat. Just as it would seem all hope was lost, the disciples wake up Jesus, and He calms the storm by speaking to the winds and waves. Then He reprimands His followers with these words: "Why are you so fearful? How is it that you have no faith?" (Mark 4:40). Translation: "I would expect this kind of behavior from those who don't know Me, but you know that I wouldn't bring you out here to die. You know that I have the power over nature. You've seen Me work more than just a few miracles, and, by the way, I told you before we began that we were going to other side." Christ was upset because considering how well they knew Him, they should have trusted Him more.

Do you know where courage comes from? Trust. David had the courage to face Goliath because he trusted in what he had seen God do in the past. He had seen God use his slingshot and staff to kill the bear and the lion. Why should this pagan loudmouth be any different? If you are going to do your natural part to bring about a supernatural turnaround and revolutionize the world you live in, then you will need to develop a sense of trust in who God is—and that comes through relationship.

A third thing God wants you to demonstrate in your natural work is cheerfulness—*joy*! The world is lacking a good old-fashioned sense of joy. The Bible says, "God loves a cheerful giver" (2 Corinthians 9:7). Why? Because when you work cheerfully, it means you really want to do it. Everyone knows what forced labor looks like. Just picture a teenager who is being made to clean his room. There is not a lot of cheer there. Joy is one of the natural things that should be seen in the lives of all individuals who consider themselves children of God. If you don't have joy, then you don't have Jesus. You may have religion, but you are not walking in relationship with Him.

Understand that I am not talking about a sense of false hope and happiness that is insincere and cheap. I am talking about an undeniable reality that celebrates each and every day what God has done in your life and what you are seeing Him do in the lives of others through you. That kind of joy is the fuel behind the force that will inspire people to join your movement and create a revolution that will become a reality that cannot be stopped. You have a role to play concerning the supernatural change you want to see God make. Don't worry whether or not you are able; just remember the simple but powerful truth—"The *joy* of the LORD is your strength" (Nehemiah 8:10, emphasis added)!

Step 2.5: Recognize the Natural Half of the Supernatural

- God wants to do His miraculous work in and through the lives of men.

- He is looking for those who are faithful, willing to trust, and cheerful.

- The best way to demonstrate gratitude for the gifts and talents that you have been given is to use them right where you are.

Questions to Consider

1. Is there a place where I can begin to be faithful today, knowing God will enable me to accomplish more tomorrow?

   _____

   _____

2. Do I have the kind of relationship that creates trust in who God is and what He says I can do, or am I leaning on someone else's endorsement?

   _____

   _____

Step 2.6

NEVER UNDERESTIMATE THE SUPER HALF OF THE SUPERNATURAL

WHILE MEN ON this earth may forget to do their part, God in heaven is always doing His. He never fails! The Bible says that even when we are not faithful, He remains faithful, because He cannot deny Himself. The reason this is important to remember when considering the society we want to change is the fact that when the church finally starts to do their part of the work, change will come—because God's work is already done! Throughout Scripture you will notice that the word *if* is never applied to God; it is always about us.

> If My people who are called by My name will humble themselves, and pray and seek My face, and turn from their wicked ways, then I will...
>
> —2 CHRONICLES 7:14

> Whoever confesses Me before men, him I will also confess before My Father....But whoever denies Me...I will also deny.
>
> —MATTHEW 10:32–33

> If we confess our sins, He is faithful and just to forgive us our sins.
>
> —1 JOHN 1:9

We are the conditional beings, and He is unconditional. Therefore the question is never about God's behavior; it is always about our own. That is why you can never underestimate the super half of the supernatural.

God rewards those who diligently seek Him. That means that He is not into bailing out bad behavior; He is into honoring obedience. One of the major causes of our society's condition is that we have stopped diligently seeking the Lord. We like to consider Him available should we need Him, but if everything is OK, then we'll catch up later. Our sporadic behavior doesn't obligate God to give us unlimited blessings at our request. This behavior just takes God for granted.

The Bible talks about what a child of God can expect regarding trials. James wrote, "Count it all joy when you fall into various trials" (James 1:2). His words remind us that trials come in every shape and size. Now keep in mind there is a difference between a *trial* and a *problem*. A *trial* is something that you "fall into." A *problem* is a situation that you create. If and when you find yourself in a problem, you must take responsibility for your behavior, ask forgiveness, and begin again. When you fall into a trial, you have a reason to "count it all joy," because there is a supernatural God in heaven who is watching over you and who has promised you that this will work out for His glory and your good.

It's from this truth that Paul wrote, "We are more than conquerors through Him who loved us" (Romans 8:37). This means that although we may not be able to avoid the trouble, we will come out better on the other side. Persecution has always helped the church to grow. It purges the inconsistencies in all of us. There is nothing like trouble to make you pray, nothing causes you to focus and try like need, and nothing makes you celebrate and rejoice in the Lord like deliverance from the crisis He has brought you through.

Here are a few things you need to keep in mind about the supernatural source that is backing you up. He's much bigger than you think. So many times we want to apply natural attributes to almighty God. We think that when we're surprised, He's surprised; when we don't know what to do, He's wondering what to do also. But remember that He knew about the things you didn't see coming well in advance. The things you do know about God are those things He has been willing to reveal, and just when you think that He cannot get any better, you find out that there is more than you could imagine.

That's the dynamic power of what we call *supernatural*. We are the natural part of the equation; He makes up the super. We are to do all that is in our natural ability, and then He adds to it His unlimited ability, and what happens next revolutionizes the world. Many times when we encounter the seemingly impossible, we waste time throwing our hands in the air in despair and hanging our heads in defeat. What we should be doing is seeking the Lord, asking the all-knowing and all-powerful God, "What do I do next?" Then whatever He tells you to do, do it!

You may think it cannot be that simple, but why not? God didn't ask you to understand Him; He just asked you to obey Him. Remember that the outcome is up to Him. If God says, "Move," do it. If He says, "Stand still," then hold your ground. If He instructs you to give, then without hesitation do as you are told. To stand there and argue is to let your stubbornness replace your trust in God. People will make claims like, "Well, I just don't want to appear foolish." Of course you don't; nobody does. But here's something you need to keep in mind: faith will never make you look foolish; God will always show up and prove that you are right.

Look at Elijah on top of Mount Carmel. I am certain that he felt more than strange when the Lord told him to pour water on the sacrifice. But his faith in God didn't make him appear the least bit foolish when forked tongues of fire fell from the sky and consumed the altar until there wasn't a stone in sight. I remember my father telling me of a time when his mother did what she felt the Lord was leading her to do, and in doing so she risked appearing foolish.

She and her family were living in Houston at the time when my grandfather was a pastor. My father was about sixteen years old and had just come home from football practice as his mother was coming out the door. She headed across the alley behind their home to the neighbor's home. When my dad asked her where she was going, she told him that she had been praying and the Lord had shown her that the neighbor's son was suffering with epilepsy just as her own son had suffered. She then told my father that she felt that if she would go across the street and pray for the boy, that he too would be healed just as her older son Bill had been.

Although my father had been raised in church all of his life, at the age of sixteen he wasn't living for the Lord, and he began to try to convince his mother not to go. "Mom, come on. They are nice people; you will embarrass them!"

She replied, "John, I am doing what I believe God wants me to do."

"Mom, please come inside; you haven't even met them." He knew by now that once my grandmother's mind was made up, it was a waste of time to try and change it. He also knew that when my grandmother opened her mouth to pray, she made certain every being in heaven and on the earth could hear her. She was never one to be shy about what she believed, and she is still that way to this day.

She went over to the neighbor's house, knocked on the door, introduced herself, and explained why she had come. A few minutes later the sound of my grandmother's prayer could be heard around the block, and with the word "Amen," she walked back out of the door where she had just come, across the alley, and back to her own house. There was no immediate change in the young man's condition. About two months later the family suddenly moved, which was no surprise to my father. He felt that they did it to get away from the *Holy Roller* across the street.

Several months later, while my father and his mother were shopping at the grocery store, a woman came running down the aisle at the other end of the building toward them. "Mrs. Hagee! Mrs. Hagee! Oh, Mrs. Hagee!" The closer she got, the louder she yelled. As she reached them, both my dad and grandmother recognized her as their old neighbor and the mother of the boy my grandmother had felt led to pray for. The woman went on to tell them that from the moment my grandmother prayed, her son's condition began to improve. At his last doctor's appointment, his diagnosis had been changed to *cured*.

Faith never makes you appear foolish. It might make you feel like you're taking a risk at the time, but if the Lord led you out on the edge of the limb, you're right where you need to be—so hang on and enjoy the ride! Consider the turnaround that took place in that home all because my grandmother refused to underestimate the supernatural power of God and was obedient to His leading. Think of the revolution that took place in that young man's life. He no longer lived under the oppression of a physical dictator that controlled his health. He was free to fully enjoy life and able to share with others what the power of God had done for him. There's nothing foolish about that. Never forget this fact: we are responsible to do our part, because God has already done His. Never underestimate the super half of the supernatural.

Step 2.6: Never Underestimate the Super Half of the Supernatural

- God never fails; repeat it until you believe it.

- What takes you by surprise, He has seen all along.

- Rather than worry about your circumstance, diligently seek the Lord and do whatever He tells you to do.

- Faith will never make you look foolish.

Questions to Consider

1. Is the circumstance that I am in a trial I have fallen into or a problem that I created?

_____

_____

2. Am I seeking the Lord for the solution or wasting my time whining and complaining?

_____

_____

3. Am I willing to do whatever I feel the Lord leading me to do?

_____

_____

Step 2.7

THE VALUE OF "YES, SIR"

A s early as I can remember, there was only one appropriate response in my father's house—"Yes, sir." While it verbally demonstrated respect, it mentally became a habit that thirty plus years later I cannot escape. Even when people beg me to stop saying "Yes, sir," I find it difficult. There are times when I visit with adults and listen to younger children and wonder where this phrase went. Today you hear every form of response from "Yeah" to "Okeydokey" to "You got it" to "What's up?" But "sir" is gone. I have to tell you, I miss it. It was a verbal demonstration that asserted I was gladly under my father's total control. If society is going to change, the church has to lead the charge. For that to occur, the church must gladly demonstrate its willingness to be under complete control and embrace the value of a good, old-fashioned "Yes, sir." When we do, we will be a church under complete control.

We are referred to in the New Testament as the army of the living God. (See Revelation 19:19.) Armies are not bodies of weakness but battalions of meekness. Meekness is power under control, and that is exactly what the church should be—full of power and totally under control. Without a leader, anarchy results. So, logically speaking, Christians should take the lead because of who we are and how we function in society. After all, we were given the promise that we would be the head and not the tail (Deuteronomy 28:13), correct?

The problem that often causes people to resist the leadership that they are under is the abuse of power. This has certainly been the case in the church at times. Why is it that more dads today don't require the same "Yes, sir" their fathers did? More than likely it is the result of the resentment they have for an authority figure who abused his power.

However, if we are willing to put things back in proper order, we will find that we can be the leaders in every city and every nation of the world. We are what Christ said: the *salt of the earth* and the *light of the world*. We are agents of change. The fast way to make a change is to willingly yield control to our supreme leader, Christ the Lord.

Why salt? Salt has two functions: it purifies and it heals. When salt touches things that have been contaminated, it causes them to become clean. When the church behaves as it should, we will be able to clean up streets, homes, neighborhoods, cities, and lives. The world should be able to tell where a Christian has been and all that Christians have done. In all those places there should be evidence of a real change.

Christians are also the light of the world. Light shines and dispels all darkness. The smallest candle defies the darkness in the largest room because it is just that much more powerful than its adversary. We are not to consider ourselves in any way feeble in our faith. Our faith is indeed what overcomes the world. The question is, are we doing what we were created to do and shining against the darkness, or are we trying to entertain it and coexist?

There is a passage in Titus that is a daily challenge to me as I perform the work of the church:

> In all things showing yourself to be a pattern of good works; in doctrine showing integrity, reverence, incorruptibility, sound speech that cannot be condemned, that one who is an opponent may be ashamed, having nothing evil to say of you.
>
> —Titus 2:7–8

The challenge is so clear; we are to live the kind of lives that make those who do not appreciate us feel guilty when they have anything negative to say concerning us. When that describes the behavior in your church, the community in which your church is located will be changed forever. The city where your community is incorporated will never be the same again. The state that your city is in will be a better state, and the nation where your state is located will be a stronger and more righteous nation—not to mention that the nation you live in will make the world floating in space a better place to live.

But most importantly, you will be doing your part to create a difference right where you are. Since you are responsible for your actions and God is responsible for the outcome, then you know that when you do your part, when you say, "Yes, Sir," He'll handle the rest.

Section 2 Review: Seven Lessons That Will Change the World Around You

2.1 Put things back in place.

2.2 Work together when you can, alone when you must, but always work.

2.3 Fix the foundation.

2.4 Get back to the Book.

2.5 Recognize the natural half of the supernatural.

2.6 Never underestimate the super half of the supernatural.

2.7 Learn the value of "Yes, sir."

Questions to Consider

1. Am I doing my part in making a difference in my world?

   _____

   _____

   _____

2. When is the last time God asked and I answered with "Yes, Sir!"

   _____

   _____

   _____

Section Three

FINANCIAL RESPONSE-ABILITY

Seven Lessons of Financial Responsibility

BY NOW THE mental juices should be flowing about the many things you can be personally responsible for to make a difference in the world around you. It doesn't really matter what area of the world you want to impact; whether as an individual or as a church, it requires finances and resources to accomplish. This next section is devoted to sharing with you the financial principles I've seen my father and others use to successfully accomplish their divine purpose.

Before we begin, understand these things:

First, money is not a dirty word. Everything in our modern world is connected to it. If you are going to make a difference, sooner or later money will play a role.

Second, when it comes to finances, it's your focus that really counts. If you focus simply on the bottom line—make more, keep more, do more—you may have a big bank account, but it's only a matter of time before your financial movement fades away and someone else takes your place. On the contrary, if you focus on using finances as a tool to be of benefit to as many as possible, you will discover a river of resources that will always have you ready to respond to the needs of the world around you.

This was the very thing that Joseph did in Egypt that caused the nation to become the richest and most powerful nation on the face of the earth. By properly managing resources during the prosperous years, he was able to sustain himself and the entire nation in the lean years. In addition, he sold grain to the other nations of the world and captured their wealth by paying attention and addressing the need before they knew they needed it.

Consider also the supernatural resource involved in Joseph's prosperity. He was forewarned of what would happen through a dream that he interpreted for Pharaoh. Joseph used the supernatural gift that God had given him to accomplish the financial freedom that made him personally response-able. Had Joseph allowed the bitterness of his past to infect him, or had he let each of his setbacks create a sense of insecurity, he might not have properly interpreted the dream and not been able to achieve his destiny.

Don't let the world around you get you down. There is no shortage of difficulties in the economic environment we face, but those who pay attention to the need and are willing to use the gifts God has given them will not only *survive* in this season but will also *thrive*. In this section of the book I want to show you seven simple steps that each of us can apply to our lives that will enable us to prosper in perilous times. By properly allowing these principles to become a part of your approach to financial management, you will discover that there will never be a reason or season where you should face economic shortage again.

Step 3.1

EMBRACE THE JOY OF WORKING

ON APRIL 12, 1948, something occurred in my father's young life that would change who he was forever. He woke up on the morning of his eighth birthday filled with the excitement and expectation that this day was going to be special. He came into the kitchen where his mother was preparing the morning meal with a smile from ear to ear across his face. Right after wishing him a happy birthday, my grandmother informed my father, "Son, right after breakfast is over, I want you to get in the car with me, because I am going to give you something today that is going to change your life." My dad knew it! He was right! This was going to be the birthday to end all birthdays. Maybe he would get the Schwinn bicycle that he had earmarked in the Sears and Roebuck catalog. Maybe he was going to get a party with all his friends. The last thing he had gotten for his birthday was a cake at the age of six because family resources were very limited with three boys to raise in a small country church. Grandma and Grandpa didn't make much of birthdays. But on this day my dad knew that whatever lay ahead was going to be over the top.

Breakfast couldn't end fast enough. The car couldn't pull out of the driveway quickly enough. The excitement he felt was almost enough to make an eight-year-old boy swoon. Rather than get on the highway and turn west toward the big city of Houston, they stayed on the back roads of the country and passed by familiar fence lines and farms in the community where they lived. Finally the car came to a stop in front of a large field with crop rows of white that looked like they reached to the horizon and ended where the earth touched the sky.

My grandmother put the car in park, looked over the front seat into the eyes of her son in the back, and said words he'll never forget:

"John, today for your birthday I am going to give you something that is going to help you every day the rest of your life—a job."

My father thought, "A JOB? Where's the bike?" My grandmother had taken my father to the field of one of the largest cotton farmers in that part of the county. He was hiring day laborers to pull the cotton out of the thorny bolls where they grew. Each person would drag a hundred-pound sack behind him and at the end of the day would get paid for what he had picked. The wages were easy enough, one dollar per every one hundred pounds. This was far different from the toy he had dreamed about the night before, but the evidence of the impact that it made on his life is something that can still be seen today.

My dad was by far one of the youngest in the field, and when he began the work, he noticed that the taller workers were straddling one row of cotton and picking not only the one between their legs but the one on the right and left. Knowing he was too short to do that, my eight-year-old dad looked up at the cotton farmer who had just hired him and asked, "Excuse me, sir. How does a boy like me make his way to the other end?" The words the old cotton farmer spoke have been *impressed* upon me many times throughout my life: "That's easy, son; heads down, hinnies up!" The lesson that my father learned was the value of work. The moral that he has passed on to me is, "Son, nothing in your life will work unless you do."

Did you know that you and I were created to work? That is one of the main reasons God breathed into the dust of Eden and man became a living being—so that we could go to work. Look at what the account of Genesis says. We were created that we might tend the garden and keep it. When you consider the geographic description given in the Bible for the garden, Adam had a lot on his plate. He wasn't pruning a few rows of orchids and watering the beans. He was looking after a vast piece of real estate and was put in charge of everything. God would bring him the animals, and whatever he named them, they were called. He had to have the mind of a dictionary. Think of all that was required to keep it straight! I am at the point with just three children of asking them to wear name tags so I at least get it right half of the time.

Then consider this passage: "The LORD God made the earth and the heavens, before any plant of the field was in the earth and before any herb of the field had grown. For the LORD God had not caused it to rain on the earth, and there was no man to till the ground" (Genesis 2:4–5). The message is pretty clear: God had not put anything into production because there was no one in place to manage it. Then God created Adam, and he was put in his place and things started happening. There are things God wants to do, but He's waiting on you to get in the proper place to do it.

It's important to keep this biblical fact in mind, because many people attribute work as a part of the curse that came with sin. Not true at all. Work is something that you were created to do. You were created in the image of God, and He was *at work* and still is. What came with sin is the difficulty associated with work. Prior to Adam's fall, he enjoyed his job. Who wouldn't! Walking around with the lions and tigers in the morning and hanging out with God in the evening. With no traffic to endure in a commute and no taxes at the end of the year, Adam had it made. Then, with the *Fall* came toil and labor and thorns and thistles and dust. Sin didn't create work; sin made work something to endure.

Now, for the good news: just as Christ came to redeem man who suffered in the Fall, He came to restore all that man lost in the Fall. Therefore He can restore your joy in the work that you do. It does not have to be a matter of labor and something to endure; it can be something that you do as a sacrifice of praise unto Him. The Bible says, "Whatever your hand finds to do, do it with your might" (Ecclesiastes 9:10). Work as if God was sitting right next to you watching, and at the end of every task, behave as if you can see the smile on His face for the quality of work that you have done.

Take a moment and consider your position. Is your life like the Garden of Eden before Adam arrived? That would mean there is no production, because you are out of place. One of the main reasons that God does not cause the fruitful abundance He is capable of producing in your life to manifest is because something is out of place, and if He caused you to prosper, it would go to waste. Before you start considering what, when, and where you want the blessing of God to be poured out, make sure you are in position to make the most of His blessing when it comes. Until you do, you may find yourself filled with frustration over what you expect but will never collect.

One of the ways to make sure you are in place is to take a look at your labor-to-leisure ratio. God rested from His work on the seventh day, and when He gave Moses the Ten Commandments, He said, "Six days you shall labor and do all your work, but the seventh day is the Sabbath of the LORD your God. In it you shall do no work" (Exodus 20:9–10). This means that 85 percent of your life should be spent working. Some folks could stand to slow down and throttle back, and a few others certainly need to step it up. But the fact remains that you are expected to go to work.

Ask yourself this question: "Am I making the most of the work that I have to do?" I know so many young people who put in a half-hearted effort because the place they are working now is not the place where they want to be. Here's something my grandmother used to say: "Shame on you!" There is a very distinct word for those who are not enthusiastic about their job: unemployed! You should be thankful each and every day that you have the physical strength to get up and earn a living. The Bible says that you can eat with gladness the bread of the labor of your hands (Psalm 128:2). It is a blessed thing to have a place where you can receive an income for effort. Always make sure that the effort you give is greater than the income you receive, and you will never stop growing in what you do. It may not be the work that you want, but make the most of the work that you get.

I recently had a conversation with three young ladies who were sipping seven-dollar *venti* coffees, carrying five-hundred-dollar cell phones, and complaining about the destitute condition of their situations. They continued to repeat, "We have graduated from college, and we can't find jobs!" I patiently allowed them to repeat this tune until I couldn't take it anymore. Finally I started to respond, and their jaws hit the floor. I felt led—anointed, you might say—to remind them that indeed there may not be jobs in the particular fields where they were applying and for the amount of money they thought they were worth, but there was plenty of work to be found if they were willing to stop complaining and go find some.

They were not paying attention to the natural void that was being created around them. There were signs hanging in the window of every diner up and down the street where we were standing, stating "NOW HIRING ALL SHIFTS."

"*What? Restaurants? Us?* Excuse me, but we have college educations!"

So I thought, "OK, in that case I will say it real slow, or should I write it down? Stop whining and go to work!" Work creates opportunity. No one has entitled you to a job, but if you make the most of every job you have, who knows what heights it will take you to?

What if one of those young ladies had walked into any of those restaurants and informed the manager, "I am going to become the most valuable employee in this place. I am going to come to work every day ready to do whatever it takes to help this establishment succeed. I'll help look for ways to cut cost. I will fill the gaps that other employees or unforeseen situations create. At night when you shut out the lights and close the doors, you are going to say to yourself, 'I couldn't do it without you!'" There's no telling what kind of difference that approach would make. But this much is certain: it would be better than filling the air with complaints all day and going home unemployed at night.

If you want to make a difference, then that attitude of entitlement must die. For some strange reason, there is a generation who walks around believing that they are owed what they haven't earned. Only by proving your value time and time again do you become priceless. The time has come to stop looking for a way to resolve the problem from the outside and resolve to solve the problem from within. We need a good dose of the old-fashioned attitude that states, "If it is going to be, it is up to me!" When you make up your mind to become an asset to someone or something else, then you have taken the first step to becoming financially responsible.

No matter who you are, or how much or how little you have, the *free ride* is a one-way ticket to poverty. Only by work and effort do you develop the skills that you need to survive. Think about the domesticated animals you find in city zoos. They live by entitlement. Because they are confined and under the care of their keepers, they are entitled to breakfast, lunch, and dinner—all in supervised quantities and nutritional amounts. They have free health care. They are given hours of the day when they can be in certain places and then told when to return to their cages at night. I always think that it is humorous and somewhat ironic when activists' groups protest that these poor animals be allowed to return to the native environment from which they came. The very request is a death sentence from those who think they are saving the creatures' lives.

These animals have totally lost their ability to survive any other way due to all of the entitlements received while in the zoo setting. Should you release these creatures that have become acclimated to the *free ride* into a world where they have to go and fend for themselves, they would stand or walk in a circle about the size of their cages until they starved to death waiting for someone else to show up with the answer. This is a behavior not all that dissimilar from that of the three young adults standing in the parking lot whining about what they deserved and were unable to find.

The road to an economic turnaround is paved with responsibility. The greatest testament of responsibility is a willingness to work. It will create opportunity that you never dreamed imaginable and give you the skills you need to survive and thrive even in the most perilous times.

Step 3.1: Embrace the Joy of Working

- Nothing will work until you do!

- It may not be the work you want, but make the most of the work that you have.

- Sooner or later, the *free ride* leads to poverty. The mind-set of entitlement must die!

Questions to Consider

1. Am I in a proper position to receive the increased production that God can bring to my life?

   _____

   _____

2. What opportunities can I create for myself and others through a willingness to work?

   _____

   _____

3. Do I have the right attitude about work? Is it a blessing that I was created to do or a labor that I must endure?

   _____

   _____

Step 3.2
LIVE TO GIVE

THERE ARE TWO approaches to financial management when things get tight. One will cause you to clutch and cling all the more intensely to everything that you want to maintain, creating a lot more stress, which in turn leads to an entirely different list of problems. The other approach will put you in a position to obtain more than you would have ever dreamed. One is called *clinging*, and the other is called *giving*. Clinging is what one does when needing to hold on to a life raft; I, for one, hope and pray that I never find myself in that position. Giving is what one does when he or she is prospering or preparing to prosper. I want to always to be in these situations—prospering or preparing to.

It is a fact that your ability to possess more will be determined by what you are willing to turn loose. I have heard this principle taught in many ways, but the one that I relate to the most goes like this: God gives you something good. It is something that you are indeed in need of and something you cherish and hold on to with all your might. God, being the wonderful Lord that He is, wants to give you something better, but you just got comfortable holding on to what you think is really good. It is at this moment that you can either choose to cling and clutch to what you consider good, or you can let good go, give it away, and then lay hold of what is better than what you had.

Some choose to cling; others choose to let go. The thing that gets really interesting is to watch what happens to those who choose to let go and allow God to give them something better. Sooner or later, God, being the truly marvelous and loving Father that He is, brings you the absolute and very best—and guess what? It starts all over again. In order to receive what is in His hand for you, you have to give what is in your hand to Him. I can assure you that, after seeing this principle lived out in my life over and over again and watching it happen to others, you will never be disappointed. God will not let you down.

One of the reasons that we have a hard time turning loose and giving is because many people measure wealth by the quantity in life, not the quality of life. What good is all the money in the world if you cannot afford the peace to sleep at night? What real profit do you have if your every material need is met beyond your wildest dreams but you don't have anyone to share it with or to leave it to? I have seen a great number of people reach for more than they needed and lose everything that they had, rather than enjoy what they had and consider themselves rich because they had all that they truly needed.

When you recognize that one of the greatest treasures in life is to see what powerful things you can do when you give, you'll get addicted to it. When you see the hope you can bring to those who are battling hopelessness, when you watch someone's outlook on life change before your very eyes, you may indeed wonder, "Why didn't I do this earlier?"

There are two main reasons that you should give. The first is to see others made better. You are not trying to enable them to stay where they are; you are trying to help them advance. You want the gift to be a source of empowerment, not a handout that leads the recipient back down the road of entitlement. You want those whom you have blessed by giving to be inspired to give to others in the same way you have given to them. That way a giving movement that begins as a result of your actions becomes a force and, finally, a revolution that cannot be stopped.

The second reason you give is to demonstrate that the cancer of greed has not consumed your soul. My father taught his children that greed is indeed a cancer. If it exists in your life and goes untreated, it will continue to spread until you cease to give altogether, and the moment you stop giving, you start financially dying. The best way to combat greed is to give. Give with joy! Give with the knowledge that what you are letting go of wasn't yours to keep anyway. Give knowing that when you do, you are getting in a position to receive, not from the hand of man, but from the hand of God.

In the New Testament we read, "It is more blessed to give than to receive" (Acts 20:35). Why? Because when you are the recipient, you are taking from the hand of another man. When you are the giver, you are placing what is in your hands into the life of someone else, so that God can place what is in His hand into your life. When you live your life looking for ways in which to give away what you have to others, then you become a candidate to receive more than you can contain. When you begin to receive more than you can contain, all those around you are abundantly blessed as well.

Have you ever seen the pyramids of champagne glasses set up at fancy parties and receptions? They stack the glasses in such a way that they are layered from bottom to top. At the top is one glass, and each level beneath has more.

When the moment arrives to begin pouring, they start with the top glass. When it can no longer contain the volume, the drink begins to spill over into the glasses beneath; then when they are full, the next level begins to receive, and on it goes until every glass is full from the top to the bottom. And it all started with one six-ounce vessel.

You are a vessel. You are a vessel that has the ability to receive from the unlimited resource of God Himself. Don't try and keep what you cannot contain. Allow all that He pours into you to flow out of you so that He might continue to fill you until the world around you has received. When you do, the celebration will have just begun, because when you give away what God has given to you, there is always more where that came from.

Step 3.2: Live to Give

- The amount you are able to possess will be determined by what you are willing to give.

- You cannot give away that to which you are firmly clinging.

- Give to empower others, not to enable them.

Questions to Consider

1. Am I a giver?

_____

_____

2. Has greed begun to grow in my life, and if so, what am I going to do about it?

_____

_____

Step 3.3

BE FREE INDEED

EVERY ONE OF us has heard that old sales pitch, "This is the last time that you will ever find this offer anywhere!" The desire to make a sale will cause people to say and do some of the craziest things. Sales pitches like these cause people to make an impulsive financial decision that many times leads to an economic prison of debt. A very sound principle to live by is this: If it is on sale today, wait and see what they offer tomorrow. Chances are, there will always be an opportunity to have what you want in the future.

There is no place where this point is any better illustrated than by the vendors you meet in the streets of the nation of Israel. They are always making the claim, "One of a kind!" And the reality is that the backpack they are carrying is full of more of the same. Our ministry has traveled as a group to Israel for more than thirty years, and in that period of time we have seen and heard some unbelievable stuff. "Real stones from Jesus's tomb!" "Olive branches from the tree where Jesus knelt and wept!" "Rocks and sling shots just like the ones that David used!" On and on it goes from tour stop to tour stop, day after day, until it is rather comical.

Don't get me wrong; there are some truly beautiful things to buy from the nation of Israel, and historical and biblical antiquities that you would not believe, but you need to be wise about where you go and with whom you deal. On one particular trip there was a man who considered himself a real bargain hunter. If he bought something, it must be at the absolute lowest and best price. As it is all over the world and in every market, there were items that were the genuine article that cost a little more, and then there were imposters that tried to pass on something as legit for a small discount.

Our friend, the bargain shopper, couldn't help himself, and he haggled about the price of everything. I think the locals considered him to be quite entertaining. The one prize he truly wanted to claim on his trip was a sheepskin rug covered with wool that had the Star of David stitched on it. Every time the man saw one, he would plead with the guide to stop the bus. Every day he would search from store to store and vendor to vendor, unwilling to rest until he claimed his treasure.

The head guide for our tour, whom we have known for years and in many ways consider as family, was gracious enough to take this man aside and tell him that he knew exactly where to find a genuine rug covered with real wool at a fair price for its quality, if he would only be patient enough to wait a few days until the tour stopped there, and he would be able to see it. Well, the day came, and the tour bus stopped at the store. The merchandise was viewed and the price quoted, and then the haggling began. The store owner got an earful about everyone in the whole country who had the same product for far less, and unless he was willing to come down in price, there would be no deal made.

The store owner assured the man he could go no lower; the rugs were indeed genuine wool and of such quality that they could not be reduced another dime or shekel. He demonstrated enough sincerity that many on the tour bought one of the wool-covered rugs and were pleased with the product and the price. The bargain shopper, feeling he in some way had overcome all the others by resisting the offer, went right out in the street and bought the first knockoff rug he saw for a few dollars less than the price of the genuine article he had just seen in the store.

When he returned to the bus, he began to strut down the aisle informing his fellow travelers what his discriminating eye had found and his keen sense for a bargain had bought. He claimed that if the others on the bus wished to have one, he would approach the man with whom he'd struck the deal and see if there were any more of such value to be had. Somewhat perturbed by this behavior, our guide and friend made an announcement to the bus.

"You do not want to take this deal, because the rug he has is a fake, and the ones you purchased in the store are real." Incensed by the claim, the bargain shopper demanded proof or an apology. The guide very calmly and very plainly said, "Proving I'm right is as easy as a flick of my finger."

"How's that?" came the man's irritated reply.

The guide went on to explain a known fact about genuine wool versus synthetic material. Genuine wool will not burn; it is flame resistant. Synthetic material will go up in smoke like a roman candle. With that the guide walked down the aisle with a lighter in his hand and with one spark and flick of his finger set the man's knockoff rug ablaze.

The bus full of tourists did all they could not to laugh. But almost as if right on cue, a shepherd walked by with about a dozen sheep, and one of them let out the loudest "Baaa" you ever heard in all of your life. At that point, my friends, the laughter rolled like thunder and could not be contained. The moral of the story is that this man is not the only one who has ever been made to look sheepish by a deal that was just too good to resist. There are a lot of people who suffer from a very similar phenomenon every day.

Some purchase a new car they don't need because "the dealership is just giving them away!" They buy furniture they can't fit into the house because "everything must go!" Now they have to rent storage. They sign bank notes for homes they cannot afford because "the opportunity will never be this good again." And before the ink dries on the paper, they have managed to incarcerate themselves underneath a mountain of debt that becomes the dictator of their lives. Their dreams are going up in smoke because they were not based on reality but rather on a clever sales pitch that turned into an economic prison sentence. In order to know what it's like to have financial freedom, you are going to have to avoid debt at all costs, for he who is debt free is free indeed.

When God spoke about the blessings and benefits of living by His Word, He said, "You shall lend to many nations, but you shall not borrow" (Deuteronomy 15:6). A few verses later He went on to say,

"If you do not obey the voice of the LORD your God, to observe carefully all His commandments and His statutes which I command you today" (Deuteronomy 28:15), you and your children will suffer greatly and others will be placed over you. "The alien who is among you shall rise higher and higher above you, and you shall come down lower and lower. He shall lend to you, but you shall not lend to him; he shall be the head, and you shall be the tail" (verses 43–44). Debt is a hindrance to your destiny. It forces you to do things you would rather not do in order to accomplish things for which there is no reward.

No one is blessed by the act of working an extra shift to pay off a credit card. You want to live the kind of financial life where you realize a return on every ounce of effort you put out. If you are working to pay off high-interest debt, you are not the beneficiary of the hours you spend working; your lender is. When you owe no man, you have a liberty that you should never want to give away.

Before you write me off as an idealist who does not deal in reality, I want you to know that there is a difference between debt and leverage. There is such a thing as financial leverage that enables you to improve your life and the lives of your family. It is all together different from debt. Leverage is an investment in your future, using dollars that you obtained today. Debt is a hole that there is no getting out of. Leverage will catapult you forward; debt will hold you back.

Consider the small business loan taken out by a man who earns enough in profit and sales to pay off the bank and to continue to sustain his life and grow his business. That is far different from the family on a fixed monthly income who digs a huge hole with credit cards for sums of money that they cannot ever hope to repay. The man who betters his family has utilized money as a tool to leverage himself into a position that he would otherwise never hope to gain. The end result of financial leverage is a position of strength. Debt always creates weakness because it lessens your ability to stay in financial control.

If you are going to be financially free indeed, you cannot simply apply the principle to debt you have. You must also consider whether you are one of those who are so bound by money that you have a difficult time spending it. If you spend money that you don't have, you are a slave to the lender from whom you borrowed. If you refuse to spend the money that you do have, you are just as enslaved, except your dictator is the dollar. Consider my father, who, as I told you earlier, picked cotton for one dollar per hundred pounds. If someone asked him to spend five dollars as a child, he would have thought he was making a down payment on the world. When you earn your money a penny per pound from the thorn-filled boll of a cotton plant, you'll think long and hard before you let go of a dime. But if you don't turn it loose and enjoy it, sooner or later it will control you, and your financial freedom will be forfeited just the same. Those who penny-pinch may look financially better on paper than those who are in debt, but they are still just as emotionally and economically bound.

A good question to ask when spending money is, "Am I going to enjoy this or lose it?" When you spend money, you are exchanging it for something else to enjoy. When you lose money, it's gone, and there is nothing to show for it. This can be applied in a number of areas of life. Consider what you are about to exchange for what you are going to spend, and see if it is worth it. For example, my wife and I have very busy and fast-moving schedules due to the demands of the church and the ministry, which make our opportunities for free time few and far between. When they come, I do not mind exchanging dollar bills for the opportunity to make the most of our time together, because my time with her is much more important than money.

I have shared that statement with a number of people, and some have responded, "Well, when my wife and I have free time, there's just no money left to go out." Now before you make the same statement, ask yourself these questions: "Why isn't there any money left to go out? Do you owe someone? Have you borrowed more than you can afford to pay back? Are the credit card companies enjoying your paycheck more than you?" If the answer to any of these questions is yes, then even though there may not be money today to take your wife out with, there could be if you were free from debt.

When you spend money on a good or service that you otherwise would not be able to enjoy, then you exchange money for something that makes your life more enjoyable and improves its quality. When money is lost, the quality of life will not improve and may indeed be lessened.

Before you spend money, there are a number of questions that are good to ask.

1. "Can I reasonably afford this?" Reasonably means that you are not going to have to significantly alter your life in order to obtain what you are about to buy.

2. "Do I *need* this, or do I *want* this?" How you answer this question may or may not impact whether or not you make the purchase, but at least you will know going into it why you did it.

3. "Is this an item that will add to or take away from my quality of life?" A few years ago it was not that common, but now I see more and more young married couples upset with each other over how much the husband likes to play video games. You may laugh at the thought, but believe me, in certain homes this battle rages. You bought a toy that you always wanted, but you spend more time with it than you do with your spouse or family. That is not adding enjoyment and quality to your life; it is actually a bigger headache than it is worth. You did say, "I do," at the altar, but not to breaking the world record high score on the PlayStation at night. I'm not preaching against Sony, Nintendo, or any other video game system, but I am suggesting you consider what

you are about to do before you do it. It will usually solve more problems than it creates.

4. "Is this something only I will enjoy, or can my friends and family enjoy it with me?" If it's an item that brings people together, it is far more valuable than anything that pulls them apart.

The man who bought the sheepskin in Israel was sucked into an emotional vacuum that he was going to prove to the world what a brilliant bargain shopper he was; instead, he was fleeced by a sales pitch and his overwhelming desire to be proven right. Under the influence, he lost financial ground rather than gained it. It's the same emotions and influences that run through the minds of those who make the impulsive decisions that create debt. Believe me, if what you want today you can't afford, then wait until tomorrow. It will either be on sale because it is outdated, or they will have a new and improved one that you will be able to purchase outright rather than go into debt to buy. By doing so, you will have the opportunity to be debt free and stay debt free indeed.

Step 3.3: Be Free Indeed

- The borrower is always slave to the lender.

- Debt is a hindrance to your destiny.

- Leverage creates strength, progress, and opportunity.

- Debt creates weakness.

Questions to Consider

1. Do I think before I spend, or do I do what I want no matter what?

   _____

   _____

2. Am I controlled in any way by money, either through the debt I owe or the resources I refuse to spend?

   _____

   _____

3. What plan can I reasonably implement to get out from under the bondage of debt?

   _____

   _____

Step 3.4

THE RIGHT OF CAPTURE

I HAVE HEARD ALL of my life that there is a river of money some-where in the world. I have never seen it, nor swam in it or drank from it, but I have indeed heard people refer to it as if it were real. The truth is, there is a lot of money that changes hands from one day to the next, and if you choose to think of it in terms of a river, then I guess the analogy fits. Here's the point: you can create a tremendous life for you and your family financially if you understand and utilize what I call *the right of capture.*

I live in an area of the world where drought is common. As a matter of fact, for the last several years the state of Texas has suffered severely from an intense dry spell. It's in seasons like this that water and the shortage thereof become a very intense and frequent topic of discus-sion. In the water laws of the state of Texas, there is something known as *the right of capture.* I'll try my best to paraphrase. The right of cap-ture establishes that if you have a source of water, say a river or a creek, flowing on your property, you have the right to divert the water and capture it, so long as you create a way for it to flow back to its source and continue to be used by others downstream.

For example, if I lived on a piece of property with a creek, I could dig a pond on my property, divert the creek to fill the pond, and then create a way for the water from the pond to overflow back into the source that it came from, in this case the creek. The right of capture enables me to create a resource out of the water; I just can't keep the resource on my property—I have to make sure I give it back.

Here's how it applies in your financial life. Each of us, at one time or another, plays one of two roles: we are either a *source* or a *reser-voir.* We are either the ones providing, or we are being provided for.

In order for us to ensure that there will always be enough resources to go around, we must be certain that we are willing to give back to the source from which we captured our provision.

It is important at this time to mention that the source of every financial resource is God. He owns it all. Look it up for yourself. He has declared, "'The silver is Mine, and the gold is Mine,' says the LORD of hosts" (Haggai 2:8). That sounds pretty clear to me. Deuteronomy 8:18 says, "The LORD your God…gives you power to get wealth." God has His own right of capture laws for you. He sends His resources into your life, and you have the opportunity to create a reservoir where those resources can be used as a blessing for yourself and those you love—but you had better ensure that you are being a blessing to someone else. In order to continue receiving, you have to continue giving back. Otherwise two things occur: One, you have violated the right of capture, and you are inviting God's financial judgment upon you. Second, if you retain all that you have been given and never give back, you will begin to stagnate, and stagnation stinks!

To better apply this financial lesson, I'll use the church my father founded as an example. Cornerstone Church is both a reservoir and a source. God has blessed us and sustains us with His provision. He has placed us in the city of San Antonio to minister to those who are committed to the church and to reach out into the community to make a difference for Him. The community of San Antonio and its citizens support the church locally. We utilize the funds that are given to the church to create resources for those who live in the community, and then we give them back to the citizens who are willing to participate in what we freely offer. In this case we are both a source of support to those who are receiving from us and a reservoir of resources for those whom God has led to support us.

We are constantly giving back to the community, because we are responsible to do so. We try to create a number of opportunities on a weekly, monthly, and annual basis to see the city of San Antonio blessed by the resources of the church. We have an inner-city outreach that enables people to be fed, clothed, and ministered to. We have a school where the tuition is greatly reduced so that families who would otherwise not be able to attend can send their children to an excellent private school and receive a first-class education. We have a ministry to single mothers. We have trips for fatherless children. We have programs to help with all areas of crisis and need and life issues, and they are open to the public. All you have to do is come on in.

Why do we do all of this? Because we are accountable to return the resource to its source. We can capture it for the purpose of running the ministry, but if we don't create a way to give it back, then we are mismanaging what the Lord has given.

Take a moment and consider how many ways this principle can be applied in your life. How many different relationships do you see yourself in as a source or a reservoir? Are you doing your part not only to properly manage what you've captured but also to give back to where it came from? A church is not the only reservoir around. You as an individual are a reservoir. God put you in a family. You took from the resources of the family to grow up and become productive, now what are you giving back to the family God gave you? I know a lot of elderly people who have a number of children, some of them with significant means, and these parents in their aged state cannot get their children to care for them. The children were reservoirs that the parents filled up with the work of their lives, and the children, for whatever reason, refuse to give back.

The Bible says, "But if any provide not for his own, and specially for those of his own house, he hath denied the faith, and is worse than an infidel" (1 Timothy 5:8, KJV). Translation: better for you to be an unbeliever than to behave in such a fashion.

Consider the right of capture when it concerns education. Colleges and universities are sources where education takes place, and when the students graduate, they become alumni, and many of them give back to the school. Why? Because they are returning back to the source. Look at hospitals as reservoirs and resources as it applies to health care. When you see lives that are being healed by the work done by the doctors and the staff in a medical field, it is a great place to return the resource to its source. The harder you look for places to give back, the more you find.

You may be asking, "How much may I capture?" The answer is simple: as much as you need. How much need you have should determine how long you hold and use the resource before it flows back. There are two things to keep in mind concerning this matter: the size of your source and how many are benefitting from your reservoir.

Let's go back to the analogy of water. If all I had were a two-foot stream of slow-moving water coming across my property, I wouldn't dig a hole that looked like the Grand Canyon and wait for the tank to fill. On the other hand, if I had something as wide and impressive as the Mississippi River for a source, I could have as large a reservoir as I wanted, and it would be full in no time. If you look to the world as your source, you will function from a position of insufficiency. If you focus on God as your supplier, you will have an unlimited source, and the size of reservoir will be able to be a blessing to as many as you are willing to effectively try and reach with what He is able to provide. Remember: *the greater the need, the greater the provision.*

If you are constantly doing your part to meet others' needs, it doesn't matter who you are or what you are doing. Whether church work or business, you will never run out of things to do, and you will always prosper. You may capture what you require, but by giving back to the source, you ensure that there is enough to go around. Never become a place where the resource is captured and unreciprocated. If you do, you'll stagnate, and no one likes to sit by a stagnate pond. It's usually covered with scum. Look for a place to give back to the source, and see what God sends downstream.

Step 3.4: The Right of Capture

- You can capture and keep a stream of resource so long as you give back to your source.

- God is the source; make sure you are giving back in service to Him.

- When you don't give back, you have violated the right of capture and start to stagnate, and stagnation stinks.

Questions to Consider

1. Have I given back to the sources from which I received?

   _____

   _____

2. Am I using my resources to meet the needs of others or using them only on myself?

   _____

   _____

Step 3.5

START SAVING AND INVESTING: STOP CONSUMING

W HEN YOU HEAR someone say, "I've never seen it like this before," you are dealing with someone who has never looked at or studied history, especially economic history. Believe it or not, the stock market wasn't born the day you graduated from school and went to work. It has been around in one form or another for centuries. As long as goods and services have been produced and sold, there have been markets to trade them in. Anything you are watching now that concerns wealth and resource has already happened in history before.

Recently I heard a well-known expert on the economy say that he had "never seen an economic bubble before." In order for that statement to be true, he would have had to have been blind or in denial. This person had been a major player in politics and economics since the late sixties, and off the top of my head, I could name at least six so-called *bubbles* that had occurred, which I had to study about in the business courses I took at the university. There was the stock market bubble of the late 1960s, the real estate bubble in Texas, the gold bubble, the oil bubble, the Japan bubble, and the Kuwait bubble. Regardless of whether or not you understand these bubbles, the point is, this so-called expert knew better; he was just refusing to admit it. That attitude is probably the most threatening to our economic survival. Denying the problem never solves the problem.

My father taught me a lesson that is so universal in its truth it could go on any page in this book, but I choose to put it here: "You cannot change what you will not confront." The world we live in is talking about our economic problems, but rather than confront them, they are covering them up. Local governments are complaining about the cover-up, but they're not confronting them. So, if they won't confront on a large scale, we must do so on our own individual basis. The way we do this is to stop consuming and start saving and investing.

The major problem with our current economic environment is that it promotes the opposite behavior rather than investment and saving; it almost forces consumption. This is due to the already high—and ever-increasing—rate of taxation.

The moment you get a job and earn income, you start paying taxes. If you save money, no matter how small the rate, you still pay taxes on the interest you earn. If you buy a stock and have the good fortune of realizing a dividend, you pay taxes on the risk you took and the money you made. If you sell real estate, you pay taxes. When you die, your estate will have to pay taxes. Should you live long enough to receive a social security income, once again you will pay taxes. Forget the fact that you previously paid the taxes to social security back when you got a job and started earning income. It's this kind of an environment that encourages you to consume what you earn today rather than save some for tomorrow and make investments that will benefit you and your family in the long run.

This needs to change. When it does, it will cause an economic revolution.

Right now there is another bubble forming. It is the consumption bubble. It is driven by people who purchase on credit what they hope to be able to pay for tomorrow. When this bubble bursts, it will make all other bubbles seem like a carbonated soft drink compared to the economic eruption that takes place. Of course, it may not be what you want to hear, but there is a flood coming, so start building the ark today. Stop consuming, and start saving and investing. You must be response-able when it happens, which means you have to be responsible today.

When you study history, you find that people do not give up their general beliefs easily, no matter what their circumstances are. Consider Columbus. History states that some of those who sailed with him were criminals sentenced to the voyage because it was believed that the moment they sailed off of the edge of the earth, at least the crew would not be missed. Even Columbus himself maintained two maps and two logbooks—one for the crew to see and one for himself in the event he was wrong and the world was flat.

One of the most common and dangerous general beliefs of this generation is that you can actually get something for nothing; that somehow, someway, someone will provide all that you have ever dreamed of or imagined. I recently saw a street interview conducted at random with a nineteen-year-old girl. With a straight face and serious expression she told the interviewer that she was going to be both rich and famous and that she would be able to retire from her career and enjoy life at the age of twenty-nine. What was she doing for a job to be on such a fast track, you ask? Absolutely nothing. She didn't work; she didn't go to school; she was simply waiting to be discovered.

Such behavior can only be demonstrated by individuals who do not make decisions with their heads. They may be starry-eyed dreamers, but they are not thinkers. Look at history and tell me where you see a time that anyone made anything by spending. It has never happened, nor will it ever happen. We have been duped as a society into believing words like *stimulus* and *bailout* can really resolve the problem. The truth is that it only makes it worse. By printing more money, the government makes the dollar in your pocket today worth less than it was yesterday and creates an atmosphere where you can buy only less with what you have. Such thinking is the opposite of wealth building and prosperity and is, as a matter of fact, a paved road to poverty.

Because we are heeding the advice of those who are divorced from reality, we know as much about the economic future as those who are making scientific guesses on the psychic hotline. Some will say, "Well, the numbers won't lie." They do when liars write them down! The only way to be able to ensure any measure of future financial well-being is to take action today and trust God for tomorrow. Confront it while you can, because if you don't, it will be too late.

Begin by losing the herd mentality. In times like these you need to take account of what works *for you* and keep doing it. Stop trying to maintain pace with your peers. Just because they are unwilling to cut back on spending in their home doesn't mean it's a bad idea at yours. As I said earlier, you have to build an ark.

The first step to building an ark is to hear and believe the warning of the approaching flood. Noah didn't start on his construction project until he heard and believed what the Lord told him concerning the future of the world. Before you take action of any kind on anything, you must hear and believe the warning.

Then Noah gathered his materials. The Lord gave him exact plans for what he was to do and told him the exact materials that he was to do it with. The consumption bubble that is about to burst will be caused by inflation; therefore you need to financially gather the materials that will guard against such conditions. This may include a diversification of your funds into things like gold and real estate, if you have the opportunity to acquire them. At this moment gold is at an all-time high, and dirt is at an all-time low. I think that history will again prove that getting in on the bottom and riding to the top beats the alternative.

The third thing that Noah did was to stay true to the plan. It took one hundred twenty years before the weather in Noah's life changed, but when it did, he was thrilled that he had been a wise builder. I cannot tell you with any amount of certainty when the real economic trouble is coming, but I can tell that what we are going through now may seem to be the beginning of sorrows, but it doesn't compare to what's on the horizon. The sooner you put your plan in place to stop consuming and start saving and investing, the better off you will be.

Finally, Noah got on board and rode out the storm. What good would it have been for Noah to invest all of that effort and resources in compiling the materials and doing the years of labor had he not gotten on board? I have seen people manage their resources with wisdom and stewardship for a long period of time, and then all of the sudden do the one thing that you least expected them to do. This kind of random behavior betrays the years of investment you made and can cost you and your family more than you are willing to pay.

I am not a financial advisor, and I can't tell you what's going to work for you in this environment because I don't know your situation. But what I can tell you is that history has a tendency to repeat itself. Those who heard the warning, made a plan, and stuck with it survived; those who didn't begged for mercy. And we are guaranteed in the Word of God that it will happen again, for it is as Christ said: "But as the days of Noah were, so also will the coming of the Son of Man be" (Matthew 24:37).

Step 3.5: Start Saving and Investing: Stop Consuming

- Denying the problem never solves the problem.

- You cannot make money by spending it.

- You cannot get something for nothing.

Questions to Consider

1. Am I paying attention to history, taking action on what I see, and heeding the warning?

_____

_____

2. Do I have a plan in place to stop spending and start saving and investing?

_____

_____

Step 3.6

KEEP IT SIMPLE

A S COMPLEX AS life may seem, I always watched my father do what he did for simple reasons. He preaches as he does because the Word of God and its divine call require it. He works as he does because that's what it takes to support all that is before him. He addresses a need and becomes involved in a cause because it's the right thing to do. I've always appreciated the simple nature of how he lives his life, because it makes success much more measurable and every day more enjoyable. If you are going to enjoy financial success in your life, you need to be responsible to *keep it simple*. For a moment, consider the billion-dollar industry devoted to money management and finance. It is based on the *complexity* and *mystery* of money. Its customer base is comprised of people who have the ability to make money but are clueless as to what to do with it. For some reason, money, finance, and economics have become a social enigma that everyone wants to solve without looking at the evidence. The best advice that I can give to those who are looking for financial clarity is, "Keep it simple!"

Use simple words when making financial decisions, like *yes* and *no*: "Yes, I would like to buy that." "No, I cannot afford that." These are much clearer and easier to understand for both you and others than, "Well, we'll see," or "What other options do you have?" When you are vague and indecisive, you make yourself appear vulnerable and an easy target for anyone. When you are clear and confident about what you want, you usually get it.

Not only do you need to keep your answers simple, but your financial principles need to be simple as well. Confusion is much more expensive than clarity. Utilize simple rules. One simple rule my father ingrained in me that his mother instilled in him is, "If your outgo is more than your income, then your upkeep will be your downfall." Said another way: *live within your means*; don't spend what you haven't made yet. While you may consider that elementary advice, many have yet to master it.

The economic turnaround that you are looking for is not a *chance*; it is a *choice*. As long as you have embraced the joy of working and are willing to manage your money wisely, financial failure cannot happen in your life without your permission. By your actions every day you make the decision to live in financial freedom or in the prison of poverty. Here are seven choices that will keep you from experiencing financial prosperity.

Choice 1: Make your purchases using high-interest credit cards.

There has been a mountain of information gathered and given on this topic, to the extent that you can drown in the avalanche. What I can tell you is what my wife and I do. We have one credit card, and we are always shopping for a lower interest rate. Should we choose to purchase anything on that credit card, the entire bill is paid off to a zero balance at the end of the month. Only when it's down to zero does it mean you owe nothing. It's not always a fun check to write, but it's the months that sting a little that keep you mindful of what you are doing.

Choice 2: Become guarantor on a loan for anyone other than yourself.

The Book of Proverbs says, "He who is surety for a stranger will suffer, but one who hates being surety is secure" (Proverbs 11:15). That biblical warning was written by the wisest and richest man in the world for a reason. When you sign your name to pay for what someone else wants to borrow, you are surrendering control of your financial future to another, and they are now playing the role of a financial dictator in your life.

Choice 3: Steal from God.

There is a very important financial principle that involves the topic of tithing. Tithing was established in the Old Testament by Abraham and is something that God expects and commands of every man. Tithing is a characteristic that you find in those who prosper in what they do. Tithing is giving 10 percent of your income to the Lord. It is not your income; it is His. Tithing is not the payment of something you owe; it was never yours to begin with. Until the principle of tithing becomes a reality in your life, you are never going to prosper.

In the Book of Malachi the Lord goes so far as to say: "You are cursed with a curse, for you have robbed Me" (Malachi 3:9). The curse is that you will not prosper. You might think that you are getting ahead, but you're actually way behind. I've had people argue with me over this until they are red with anger and blue with exhaustion, and to be fair, arguing with me is a waste of time. This is not my principle; it is God's. Something that is very simple, very true, and easily measurable in my life and the life of others is this: you can do a lot more with the 90 percent that God has blessed than you can with the 100 percent that He's cursed.

Choice 4: Steal from another man.

The Lord never honors dishonest gain. When you take advantage of other people and are profiting from it, you may not stand guilty in a court of law here on this earth, but God the Supreme Judge in heaven holds you fully accountable.

Consider Zacchaeus in the Book of Luke. After he has met with Jesus and decided to become a follower of Christ, he makes this statement: "If I have taken anything from anyone by false accusation, I restore fourfold" (Luke 19:8). He was a tax collector for the Roman government, and it was a very common and accepted practice for tax collectors to take more than Rome required. Anything that they collected over the mandatory amount they could keep for themselves. What Zacchaeus was doing was perfectly fine within the culture he lived in. However, the moment he chose the Lord, he stopped living by the social standard and started living by God's standard. Immediately he returned, with interest, all that he had taken, knowing that only by changing his behavior on the outside could he prove he was a new man on the inside.

Theft is much more common than you think. Just one example is in the workplace. People take what isn't theirs from others all the time. Forget office supplies—what about coming late, leaving early, a full-day's pay for a half-day's work? You may think it's to your advantage, but I assure you, you will lose every time. Zechariah 5:3 says, "This is the curse that goes out over the face of the whole earth: 'Every thief shall be expelled.'" Choices have consequences, and choosing to take what isn't yours is a choice for poverty every time.

Choice 5: Be lazy.

I know it may be hard to believe based on the day in which we live, but God's Word says, "If anyone will not work, neither shall he eat" (2 Thessalonians 3:10). Why? Because hunger is a great motivator to get up and go to work. In the Book of Ruth you read that Ruth was gleaning from the corners of the field. Ruth was a widow and taking care of an aged mother-in-law. She lived in poverty and needed assistance to eat. The Law of Moses demanded that every crop producer leave the corners of his field uncut at harvest time so the less fortunate who needed something to eat could glean the corners. The point is: there was assistance for those who needed it, but they had to work in order to get it.

Laziness is a sin! God designed for you a magnificent machine in the form of your body. All of the genius of God was interwoven in the systems and functions of the body to create, burn, and store energy so you can get up and go to work. "The soul of a lazy man desires, and has nothing; but the soul of the diligent shall be made rich" (Proverbs 13:4). The best choice you can make is to get up and go to work!

Choice 6: Be wasteful.

There is a fortune in the fragments of what we often throw a way. Before you discard something as useless, ask yourself what you might do with it to bless someone else with just a little more effort on your part. If you take a moment and consider what you throw away—not in terms of trips to the garbage but dollars and cents, you may shock yourself at what you find.

Choice 7: Express an Anti-Semitic attitude.

Consider the promise of Genesis 12:3: "I will bless those who bless you, and I will curse him who curses you." If it is your desire to live by heaven's standard, then being a blessing to the nation of Israel, both as a giver and as a believer, will revolutionize your life. Don't think for a minute that I separate the success of this ministry from its unwavering support for Israel. If you want things to turn around for you in ways you never dreamed or imagined, start giving to Israel.

Just as these seven choices will lead to poverty, there are choices you can make that will lead to prosperity.

- Be faithful with the work of your hands.

- Be faithful in your church and community.

- Be faithful to the Word of God.

- Be faithful to His chosen people.

If you keep it simple, it will work every time.

Step 3.6: Keep It Simple

- Confusion is more expensive than clarity.

- Unless I allow it, failure cannot occur in my life.

- Faithfulness to God's standard brings His promises to my life.

Questions to Consider

1. Do I have a clear and concise financial plan that I understand and that can be simply communicated to others?

   _____

   _____

2. What choices am I making that are leading to poverty?

   _____

   _____

3. What choices am I making that are leading to prosperity?

   _____

   _____

Step 3.7

DEPOSIT OR WITHDRAWAL?

DID YOU KNOW that God is the president of *the* global bank? Proverbs tells us all we need to know about it: "The wealth of the sinner is stored up for the righteous" (Proverbs 13:22). This verse tells us that there are two kinds of customers in God's bank. The first group works as hard as the second group, but they have these distinctions:

1. They are wicked, and they do not accomplish God's will and purpose for their financial resources. Because of this behavior, they are only allowed to make a deposit in God's bank. They never make a withdrawal. The verse clearly states: "The wealth of the sinner is stored up..." In banker terms, it's for deposit only.

2. The second customer in God's bank lives for Him and is responsible personally, spiritually, and financially. When he goes to God's bank, he has permission to make a withdrawal.

Which kind of customer are you, and what rights and privileges do you have with the Provider?

While prosperity and financial well-being certainly have a number of factors that impact the reality of your life, they are not the result of a campaign promise or of a tax increase or decrease or of bull markets on Wall Street and around the world. Prosperity comes as the end result of the blessings of God. You may have the greatest plan and invest in the greatest economy in the world, but were it not for God's grace and His favor, you would not prosper.

People in the financial world like to talk about creating wealth. Anytime you mention the word *create* or any form of it, you need to know that you must be referring to God. He is and has always been the only Creator. Men do not create anything; we can *cause* a great number of things, but we are not creators. We can cause a man to prosper by taking what someone else has and giving it to him, but we have not created wealth—we've just redistributed it. The only place that wealth can be meaningfully created is from the Creator Himself, and that is God.

The verse in Deuteronomy that declares, "It is He [the LORD] who gives you power to get wealth," also says, "You shall remember the LORD your God" (Deuteronomy 8:18). The reason these words were written is because people forget from time to time where their financial well-being comes from. There is nothing wrong with prosperity, as some would have you to believe. Certain folks get so pious about the topic of finance that they become so heavenly minded they are no earthly good.

If it was wrong for you to prosper, would God have made Abraham rich in both land and cattle? Would Solomon have been the wealthiest king on the face of the earth? Would caravans of resources travel to find Christ in Bethlehem? Would the psalmist have written, "Let the LORD be magnified, who has pleasure in the prosperity of His servant" (Psalm 35:27)? One of the distinctions that God uses to separate His children here on Earth is prosperity. When you live according to His financial standard, your economic life will be revolutionized, because He gives you permission to make a withdrawal from His powerful resources.

Because God is the Creator, He has the ability to do what no other can—He can make more. In His Word He has promised a fourfold blessing on those who live by His financial standard. "Give [that's the standard], and it will be given to you: good measure, pressed down, shaken together, and running over [fourfold]" (Luke 6:38). You may say, "I just don't know how that's possible." If it was anyone else stating that, it wouldn't be possible. But because it is God, all things are possible. He created the heavens and the earth out of nothing in seven days, and He can create all the resources that you need without fail.

In order for this truth to create the turnaround in your financial life, you must become *seed driven* and not *need driven*. When you view your economic situation from the perspective of a long list of needs, there will never be enough resources to go around. But when you see the resources that you have as seed, then there will always be a harvest in store to meet whatever needs you may have. The concept of seedtime and harvest isn't new, by any stretch of the imagination. As a matter of fact, God established it in Genesis in covenant with Noah: "While the earth remains, seedtime and harvest...shall not cease" (Genesis 8:22).

Here are some principles to keep in mind regarding seed.

1. You cannot expect anything at harvest time if you don't sow seed. There are a lot of people looking for what they don't have coming because they have not been responsible to do their part.

2. You will reap in conjunction with what you sow. If you sow in great volume, you will reap in great volume. I often have people ask if they should give off the net or off the gross. My standard response is, "If you want to pencil whip God, don't be surprised when He does the same to you." The Bible tells us that God gives liberally. I would suggest that you do the same.

3. You cannot plant peas and expect corn. You get back what you put in.

4. When what you have doesn't meet your need, it then becomes your seed. Plant it and prepare for the harvest. The Bible tells us God is the one who provides seed for the sower (2 Corinthians 9:10). If you plant your seed,

then when you reap, you will have more seed to sow.
There are two things you can do with seed: eat it or
plant it. If you plant it, you'll always have plenty to eat.
If you eat it, you'll have nothing left to sow.

The creation of wealth comes from the Creator Himself. He gives by creating the seed. He provides the harvest. He watches over the work that you have done and rebukes the devourer for your sake. There is no limit to what He is able to do for you. He is your source—don't forget where prosperity comes from.

Let me see if I can bring multiple lessons together with this application. In the mid-1990s, my father was traveling the country preaching a series of camp meeting services titled, "Take America Back." The auditoriums and stadiums were filled with enthusiastic people who were not pleased with the spiritual and moral directions of the country, and the events were creating quite a stir.

One afternoon the phone rang in San Antonio, and the voice on the other line was one of the leading pastors in the nation whose church was located in the inner city of Los Angeles. He had heard about the "Take America Back" rallies and had one simple request: "Please come to the inner city of Los Angeles, rent an auditorium, and host a rally. We need to hear that message."

Pastor Hagee indeed felt compelled to do just that based on the sincerity of the request. It was because of his hard work that others were coming into agreement with the pro-family, pro-faith, pro-America message, and a *movement* had begun.

The difficulty of the request was not a physical one or spiritual one; it was a financial one. Because of the rental costs and the unions and labor laws in California, everything involved in the Los Angeles Camp Meeting came at a premium. The rentals were considerably higher, and because of the economic income level of inner-city Los Angeles, the financial support was significantly lower.

Do you recall the section on the *natural* half of the *supernatural*? Every night for three straight nights every seat in the Shrine Auditorium in downtown Los Angeles was packed. About one-third of the audience was churched and about two-thirds unchurched. Every altar call was saturated with individuals whose tear-filled eyes, tattoos, piercings, and broken expressions told you all you needed to know about the impact that was being made in their lives and in the community as a whole.

When the event was over, Pastor Hagee and the ministry team returned home to take account of what had been accomplished. Souls were saved, lives were changed, and the message was more than well received. However, it had come at a price that threatened the financial future of the ministry. So much had been given to the event with so little received in return, it left my dad with lots of questions and not too many answers.

In his life, when he came into such times, he called his mother. (I'm glad to know I'm not the only Hagee who leans on a parent.) My grandmother has never been one for wordy conversations, so my dad kept it brief. He shared with her the success of the event—the salvations, the healings, the services—but then he shared the downside. "Mom, it cost so much and we received so little, I've got some tough decisions to make if something doesn't happen soon."

Her response was brief and very direct. "Son, did you go *for you*, or did you go *for the Lord*?"

"I went for Him, Mom."

"Then it's His expense; He'll handle it as He sees fit. You've done your part; let God do His." Remember, I said that faith will never make you foolish.

Two days later the chief financial officer of the television ministry came to see my father with some strange news. He received a phone call from a man in Houston who expressed that he had never watched the program before that day and had actually turned it on by accident. He was not a Christian, didn't like television preachers, and had never done anything like that before, but for some reason he wanted to send the ministry "some help." He also made a point to let us know that when the help arrived, he didn't want to be called or contacted with a thank-you or to be added to any mailing list or hear from us again.

All my father said in response was, "Let's wait and see what happens." Two days later the CFO was back, this time with an envelope and these words: "Pastor, the help arrived." In his hand was a personal check for one million dollars! Believe me, his words were met with a shocked expression. This was more than enough to cover the cost of the event in Los Angeles and to keep the ministry moving forward. My father, being full of faith, said, "Let's not get too excited until it clears the bank."

One phone call later we knew the check was fully funded, and the celebration began. Immediately my dad asked for a phone number. When the voice on the other line found out who was calling, he was more than perturbed that his request for no contact was denied. He repeated that he was not a Christian, didn't go to church, and was not a believer. Just before they hung up, my father asked him, "Since this is the last time we'll ever talk, can you tell me why you did it?" His response: "I do not know; something inside made me do it and wouldn't leave me alone until I did." When he hung up the phone, my dad remembered the conversation he had with my grandmother a few days earlier: "It's His expense; He'll handle it as He sees fit."

I told you that God Almighty has a bank. The wicked make deposits, and the righteous get to make withdrawals when they need it. By being willing and able to respond to the request to go to Los Angeles, by working hard and doing all that could be done in the event, by allowing the *super* part of the supernatural to have time to work, the resources of the divine Creator were diverted and a simple financial lesson learned. "My God shall supply all your need according to His riches in glory" (Philippians 4:19).

Section 3 Review: Seven Steps of Financial Responsibility

3.1 Embrace the joy of working.

3.2 Live to give.

3.3 Be free indeed.

3.4 Exercise the right of capture.

3.5 Start saving and investing; stop spending.

3.6 Keep it simple.

3.7 Don't forget where it comes from.

Questions to Consider

1. Am I living in financial freedom, or am I held captive by a financial dictator?

_____

_____

_____

2. What are five simple things I can do to change my economic future?

_____

_____

_____

Section Four

EDUCATIONAL RESPONSE-ABILITY

*Seven Lessons That Will Change
the Future of Education*

A VERY BRIEF ANALYSIS of our current educational system will clearly establish that it is time for a response. Look at the dates printed on the sweatshirts and ball caps of some of the nation's most renowned and hallowed campuses. The year 1636 marks the establishment of Harvard University, and 1769 is the date when Dartmouth University opened its doors. In the 133-year span between the opening of these two founding educational establishments in America, there was a deep understanding that knowledge was a useless and unworthy pursuit apart from God. If you are interested in checking on my research, just look up the original charters of both Harvard and Dartmouth; they both resemble a theological thesis.

We are, without doubt, a long way from those early days. Education has taken a turn in the wrong direction, and it is time for us to turn it around. We will either revolutionize the schools, or, in the not-too-distant future, the students attending the schools will start a revolution of their own and become our dictators. The debates that take place in school board meetings across America are just one indication of what a hot topic education really is. Everyone—from the soccer mom who is dropping off and picking up her children to the politician running for reelection—has a vested interest in the information or, more appropriately, the misinformation that is being crammed into our children's heads. This is no minor issue! The impact caused by an educational system on just one generation can have a far greater and more staggering effect than anything else the students may come in contact with throughout the rest of their lives.

The moment a child's primary education begins, that child spends more waking hours with classmates and schoolteachers than with anyone else. What our children learn from kindergarten to their senior year of high school—or what they fail to learn—will be the information that they pass on to the next generation. The issues that are connected to the schoolhouse impact every other house: the church house, the courthouse, the White House, and your house. All are washed in the wake of what is being taught to our children.

The important thing to keep in mind concerning the arguments centered on education is that these discussions and debates are not about does *one plus one equal two*? There is no need to debate or argue that point—it's true no matter who you are and what you believe. The debate and battle is over your worldviews. Do you have a theistic worldview (*the belief in one God as the Creator and ruler of the universe, without rejection of revelation*) or a humanistic worldview (*pertaining to philosophical or scientific humanism*)? One view is God-centered; the other is man-centered. Currently, the man-centered view is making all the decisions in the classroom and is poisoning our children at the core. In case you think all this is just philosophical chatter, please understand that the classroom establishes what is known as accepted truth.

Forty years ago, when the majority of Americans had a different worldview, it was an acknowledged truth that lying was an unacceptable practice in any relationship and that there were *absolute truths*. Today, 94 percent of teenagers question whether the Ten Commandments are really absolute truths and believe lying is appropriate and acceptable in many cases.[1]

So when your college freshman comes home and begins to tell you that he is not sure whether the Bible you taught to him while growing up is all that relevant today, and he starts lying to you about

his behavioral habits because, even though you didn't allow such practice in your home, it is considered perfectly fine amongst his peers,
you'll suddenly care about what he's learning. The problem is, by this
point it will be too late.

This problem of truth and the humanistic worldview is nothing
new. Look in the Book of Daniel at the actions of Meshach, Shadrach,
and Abednego. They were educated in a system that had a theistic
worldview. They were taught that there was only one God and you
should have no other gods before Him. When they arrived in Babylon,
they were put into a situation where the king commanded everyone to
bow before his golden statue. This behavior is perfectly acceptable to
those with a humanistic worldview, because you'll just bend your knee
while the music plays and then be on your way.

But the Bible records that when these three brave souls heard the
sound of the trumpet, they stood ramrod straight in an ocean of those
bowing before the false god. As you know, they faced a fiery trial for
their courage, and God honored their zeal by delivering them without
the smell of smoke upon them. But there are some other lessons here
that are very important to learn concerning matters of worldviews
and education.

1. If we are going to create a change, cause a revolution,
   and be educationally response-able, we are going to have
   to take a stand, just as the three Hebrew boys did.

2. Those who do take a stand will certainly face the heat
   for their courageous decision.

3. Out of the thousands who were brought from Israel to
   Babylon and who were educated from the same book that
   these three boys were taught from, they were the only
   ones willing to stand. The message: only a few will have
   the courage to stand for the changes we must make.

Where are you in this matter? Are you standing upon your faith, ready to face the challenge, or bowing down because it's more convenient and less confrontational? I, for one, was taught that the future will be what you allow. If we allow the current condition, the outcome will be our fault, plain and simple. But if we determine that our children belong to us and not to the state, that their minds, foundations, and principles are our responsibility, then while the undertaking may be massive, the results are too precious to ignore. I want to share with you seven lessons that will change the future of education.

Step 4.1

STOP OUTSOURCING
YOUR AUTHORITY

Y<small>OU SHOULD ALWAYS</small> be the primary source of your child's education. It is your duty to maintain the role of primary influencer in their lives; anything less is negligence on your part. When I was a boy living at home, one of my favorite phrases, which I still use today, was, "My daddy said..." If I knew anything for certain, it was because my daddy told me. If I called a tree a tree, it's because my daddy told me it was a tree. If I went to church on Sunday because that was the day set aside for worship, it was because my daddy told me so. If I knew to say "Yes, sir" and "No, sir," "Yes, ma'am" and "No, ma'am," it was because my father instructed me to always respect my elders. I never had to hear anyone ask me, "Boy, didn't your daddy teach you anything?" He was, and has been, the primary influence in my life.

I have heard people ask my father, "When did you start disciplining your children?"

His standard answer: "The day they came home from the hospital."

That is not a statement of his firmness; believe me, he could be firm if needed, but it was a declaration of his dedication to seeing his children raised right. Discipline is not a matter of *when* you punish your children. Correction is a part of discipline, but discipline as a whole is *how* you train your children.

Training is a process and method of teaching that requires you to show your pupil what to do over and over again. It is through this process of repetition that the discipline is ingrained in that child's character and becomes a part of his or her habitual behavior. Your children are your pupils, your kitchen table is your classroom, and the world is your training ground. It requires a tremendous amount of commitment and dedication, but with enough classroom time and real-world application, the training will pay off, and your students will *graduate* and begin training the next generation. Proverbs 22:6 establishes this promise: "Train up a child in the way he should go, and when he is old he will not depart from it."

You should always be your child's homeroom teacher. When the teacher in the classroom, or the coach on the field, or the minister at church, or the kid down the street becomes your child's primary influencer, then something is out of place and needs to be changed. Your children do not belong to those people; they belong to you. You establish the framework for everything that they believe and will become. Have you ever seen a foundation before it is poured? There's a gridlock of boards and steel bars that determine where all of the concrete can go and what the footprint and capacity of the building will be. You are the architect of the framework of your child's life, and the Bible is the blueprint for how the building will be designed. If the educational system or the world outside pours into your child's life anything that you consider to be unacceptable, you are responsible to address it, remove it, and then teach them to reject it.

I attended both public and private schools growing up. I can tell you the good and bad of both environments. But above all else, I can tell you that no matter what I learned or was exposed to in the classes I attended, it was my father's influence that determined whether I accepted it as true or not. He was the framework that molded me. The Bible was the blueprint that is still building on the foundation my father formed.

Teaching your children brings the blessings of God into your life. Look at this truth as applied to Abraham. When God was looking for an individual with whom He could establish His covenant, He chose Abraham because He knew he would teach his children. Read the contents of the covenant that God made with Abraham: "And in your seed all the nations of the earth shall be blessed" (Genesis 26:4). How? Through Abraham's children.

The tragedy of our current situation is that we have a generation of children who have become property of the state. Their parents have outsourced their opportunity to influence their own children and instead are allowing the State Board of Education and the National Education Association (NEA) to train them. In today's business world, outsourcing is a common trend. Outsourcing is the practice of hiring out work for others to do that you can actually do yourself.

Outsourcing can create revenue because it's cheaper to have the work done outside, which saves the company time and translates into dollars, directly impacting the bottom line of budgets in corporate accounting. However, in regard to the business of family and children, outsourcing your influence to the school may save you time, but it will cost you tremendously in the long run. (The average working parent spends less than twenty minutes a day with their children.[1])

Take a look at who it is that you are outsourcing your children to. Recently, our president named Kevin Jennings as the *czar* for the oversight of *safe schools*. Following his appointment (not election but appointment), fifty-three House republicans urged the president to reverse his decision, because Jennings openly promotes a *homosexual agenda*. These same members of Congress, in a letter to the president, called Jennings "unfit to serve" and requested he be immediately removed from his post.[2] Jennings is the founder of the Gay, Lesbian, and Straight Education Network and, in his speeches and writings, has described how a high school student confided in him that he was having a relationship with an older man. Jennings's response to the high school sophomore, following his confession of the relationship, was, "You know, I hope you knew to use a condom."[3]

The newly appointed czar of safe schools has an admitted and unrepentant history of drug and alcohol abuse. Rather than see these as issues of conflict in his unelected role of oversight of the American school system, he claims that his past substance abuse "qualifies" him to help students and teachers confront those issues.[4] I assure you, this is a man whom I refuse to allow to have one ounce of influence over my children! You do not want to forfeit the future of your family to people who wish to indoctrinate them with such poison. It's unnatural. If you flush your children into that type of sewer, you have flushed your future.

Psalm 127:4 says, "Like arrows in the hand of a warrior, so are the children of one's youth." Let's apply the analogy. Arrows in the trained hand of a warrior are his method of warfare. They are the tools he uses not only to defend himself but also to defeat his enemies. Throughout this book I have referred to a number of dictators that can control your life and rob you of its quality. Children are your weapons of defense against the dictators that threaten your freedom, but you have to train them while they are young in order for this to be true.

Children can protect you against the emotional dictator of loneliness in your old age. If you have maintained a position of influence and support throughout their lives, then when you are old, your children will fill your house with the joy of grandchildren. When you train your children to be responsible, they will be your protection against poverty in your old age. My grandmother, who is ninety-seven, trained my father when he was young to work and to serve, to sow and to reap. He is now taking care of all her earthly needs, because he is a weapon against poverty in her life.

Based on some situations and depending on circumstance, it may take a great deal of effort to reestablish your influence in your child's life, but it is a work that is well worth it. You may have to turn off the TV and refuse to answer the cell phone when you get home. You may have to do things that make you and your family feel a little uncomfortable at first because they are not a part of your normal routine, but your every effort will be rewarded, and in time it will revolutionize your life and the lives of those you love the most.

This type of turnaround is so near and dear to the heart of God He promised in His Word that He would "'turn the hearts of the fathers to the children,' and the disobedient to the wisdom of the just" (Luke 1:17). This is God's way of saying, "If you have the courage to try, I will revolutionize the relationship." This type of change is one that every child is looking for. Proverbs 20:7 says, "The righteous man walks in his integrity; his children are blessed after him." You cannot separate your behavior and the quality of life that you will implant upon your children and their children long after you are gone.

The positive influence, or lack thereof, between a child and his earthly father will directly impact the influence that child is willing to receive from his or her heavenly Father. We read in Hebrews 12:9–10, "We have had human fathers who corrected us, and we paid them respect. Shall we not much more readily be in subjection to the Father of spirits and live? For they indeed for a few days chastened us as seemed best to them, but He for our profit."

The influence you have in the lives of your children is an awesome and powerful thing. It can shape the world if you focus it on the principles that are good and right, or it can destroy lives for generations if you refuse to do your job. When it comes to the family and the training of your children, outsource nothing; do it all in-house.

Step 4.1: Stop Outsourcing Your Authority

- You are to be the greatest influence in the lives of your children.

- Discipline is the process of continual training in word and deed, which will establish behavioral habits in your child's life.

- You create the structure and the form into which the contents of your child's life will be poured.

Questions to Consider

1. What are five things that I can do to establish more influence in the life of my child?

    _____

    _____

2. Have I allowed my child to become property of the state?

    _____

    _____

Step 4.2

TAKE CONTROL OF THE CAMPUS

EVERYWHERE I WENT as a child, no one had to wonder whom I belonged to. Forget the fact that I wore the man's face on my shoulders, but no matter where I went or what I was involved in, my father would come and introduce himself to my teacher, coach, or supervisor without fail. The conversations were always cordial but direct: "Hello. I am Matthew's father; if you need any assistance whatsoever concerning my son, call me!" I used to think that this was a preexisting sentence on crimes that I was yet to commit, but looking back now, as a father, I understand it was my dad's way of protecting his most important asset, me! His message was loud and clear to all forms of authority listening: "You may feel free to handle any of these other children as you would like; however, my son, that one over there, he's mine. You may not do to him anything that I do not permit." It worked like a charm.

When I would walk into a classroom, if there was ever a question about something that was going to be taught or discussed, the teacher would take me aside and ask, "Is this something that you need to talk to your dad about?" They knew if I said yes, it was better for them to call him before I got home than for both of us to show up the next day when school began for an unscheduled parent-teacher conference. Don't think it always worked in my favor. There were times when other kids were sent to the principal's office where they had the opportunity to talk their way out of trouble. But I wasn't given that same opportunity. When I needed correction, the principal wasn't necessary; my teachers would just call my father on their lunch break, and I would face the music later that night. Many intense moments of fellowship in my young life began with, "Matthew, Mrs. So-and-So called me today!"

Because of my parents' presence in my life, my teachers always knew that they either had a great partner to help in my success in education or very real rivals for the entire semester—the choice was up to them. I felt, in a way, that my parents were in control of the campus, in all matters pertaining to Matthew, that is. I can tell you that as a child it was not always the most comfortable feeling, but there are times when being a good parent and raising a good child requires you to be uncomfortable. On the other hand, looking back at what my parents did for me while comparing myself to my peers and classmates, I owe them a debt of gratitude, and the only way I know to repay them is to attempt to do the same for my own children.

You can take control of the campus in matters concerning your children, and you should do it now. The first thing you need to do is make it a point to establish a relationship with your child's teacher, no matter what grade he or she is in. When I went to college, my father had lunch with the dean before I registered as a freshman. I know you may think that is a bit extreme, but don't you think in matters concerning your children that it's time to get extreme?

If you have ever worked for a large company, you are familiar with the process of a job interview. The purpose of the interview is to make sure that you are capable of managing the assets and resources that the company will entrust to you. In your family, you are the boss, and your children are your most important asset and resource, so interview your child's teacher. Your children belong to you. They do not go where the school says they should go; they go where you say to go.

Once you have met the teacher, become a friend and an ally. Like most everything else in life, you can find those who are doing things right and those who are not. The vast majority of teachers are hardworking, caring people who receive very little assistance and resources for the huge task they have to undertake. One of the best ways to immediately become a partner for success in your child's classroom is ask the teacher, "Is there anything you need that I can help you with?"

While most schools provide some supplies to teachers, they seldom, if ever, provide all that is required for the educator to do his or her job. If you ask, most teachers can tell you about the great out-of-pocket expenses they incur every semester in order to have the tools needed to properly teach the curriculum to the class. Most teachers are on a tight personal budget, and anything you can do to help relieve some of the pressure will build tremendous bridges not only to you but also to your children while they are in the teacher's care. I am not talking about getting a Mac notebook that is better than what you have at home. I'm talking about things like pens and pencils, paper, calculators, staplers, and files. Small things, when added up, can create quite a list. You can do a little or a lot, and anything will be appreciated. You may even organize some of the other parents you know to help. Think about this: What would the atmosphere in the classroom be if the teacher came to work every day knowing that the parents of the children in that room cared enough about her to provide the supplies she needed to educate their children at no additional personal expense to her?

"Well, that's why I pay taxes!" You may think that is why you pay taxes, but that's not where the tax dollars go—but that is an entirely different subject. My point is that by doing a small act of kindness and showing generosity, you can create favor with the teacher and, in doing so, have some additional insight as to what's going on at the campus where your child spends at least eight hours every day. If you were ambitious enough, you could do something on a large enough scale to organize parents in every class, go meet with the principal, and share your ideas. Believe me, they won't say no. Then see how the attitude and behavior toward your child change. I can tell you this, when it comes time for my sons or my daughter to go to school, I want everyone on the campus watching them like a hawk and telling me what's going on.

Once you have established a favorable relationship with the teacher, begin sharing things that are important to your core values and beliefs. Let them know—without hesitation and a dramatic presentation—that there are areas where your beliefs and the current academic environment do not agree. Inform them of things that are important for you to know, large and small. Ask about things like what the curriculum plan looks like for the semester, major projects that will be due, the workload to be expected at home, feedback on whom your child eats lunch with and plays with on the playground, and how your child interacts with other children. All of this information is important in your child's life and needs to be important to you. Because we are finite and mortal, we will never be all-knowing. But in matters concerning your child and his or her school, you should give it your best shot. This doesn't mean you are always sticking your nose in where it doesn't belong. In matters concerning your child, your nose belongs there all the time! By establishing relationships with those who have the task of educating, you can obtain insight and gain access to information no one else can. This knowledge gives you control of the ground your child walks on, and that's exactly how it should be.

It is important for teachers to understand what is important to you. Their jobs are measured by whether or not your child can pass the test; your job is measured by whether or not your child can pass in life. One is a far heavier task than the other. By becoming a partner with the teachers, faculty, and staff at your child's school for a few semesters, you can make them your partners for success in your child's life.

When I was a student, there was one phrase that was often thrown around in the hallways and playgrounds: "We rule the school." It was a title competed for in the gym, in science fairs, and in other competitions. It was often applied to those who had seniority on the campus. But in my life there was never any doubt, at any time, for anyone, that even though my parents may never have come and sat beside me in class, they were with me. Everyone, from my teachers and administrators on down, knew that as far as I was concerned, my parents "ruled the school!"

Step 4.2: Take Control of the Campus

- Create a personal partnership with those who are going to educate your child.

- Be sure they know who you are and what's important to you.

- Do not be afraid to confront anything and everything that you would like to change. Your child belongs to you!

Questions to Consider

1. Am I involved enough in my child's education, and is my presence known on the campus where they attend?

_____

_____

2. What are three things I can do this semester to create a parent-teacher partnership with my child's teacher?

_____

_____

Step 4.3

SMALL VICTORIES ARE BETTER THAN NO VICTORIES AT ALL

WHEN BEING RESPONSE-ABLE in the school system, it's important that you measure success with a proper perspective. I have heard my share of impassioned speeches in both organized and spontaneous settings regarding the deplorable condition of education. These presentations often include the solution of putting prayer and the Ten Commandments back in schools. They describe an atmosphere of righteousness in the classroom that actually doesn't even exist in too many homes. I have always thought that a good rule of thumb to apply is this: before it can work in the schoolhouse, it needs to work in my house. If you don't pray with your children, why should the teacher? If you don't teach them the life principles and disciplines found in the Word of God, why should anyone else? If you think that it's the teachers' job, you're dead wrong. It's your job; the teacher's job is to supplement you.

It's important to note that any small change on the campus that you help to create represents a major victory. You may not get the Ten Commandments back on the wall or get the principal to address the school with a daily devotional or take prayer requests before class begins. However, contrary to trendy opinion, your children can pray at school right this very moment. They can read the Ten Commandments and display them on a T-shirt or a book cover or any other article of personal property like a backpack. They can organize Bible clubs and host Bible studies on the campus. You can have your child invite other children to your home, where you can be involved in the Bible study and lead it yourself. All of these may not revolutionize the national education system as a whole, but they may certainly turn your school, your community, and your child's education around.

Many who consider themselves conservative enter into what I call *all-or-nothing* conflicts. Their demands are the kinds that seek to totally destroy the opposition and will not be satisfied until they do. While we may share the same goal of complete and total change, we may need to consider that the victory will not come all at once but little by little, if we are all willing to do our part. This cooperative effort doesn't require a tremendous amount of organization, if we will loyally adhere to the same tenets of faith, biblical principles, and God-centered worldview. In military terms, a revolution would be considered *guerrilla warfare*. Guerrilla warfare, for the purpose of this book is defined as "multiple and ongoing efforts to disrupt the established system in order to create lasting change." If we are all working toward the same goal, then over time we will be successful.

Your independent effort might be to become a presence in your child's PTA. You may choose to run for the school board or start by going to a school board meeting. You may organize a parent's prayer group that meets for the sole purpose of praying for the school that your child attends. This prayer group can ask every teacher if they have any needs or concerns that they would like for your group to pray about. If they are believers and people of faith themselves, this question will help you identify your allies. If they are unbelievers and hostile to the faith, you can pleasantly look them in the eye and say, "We are praying for you just the same."

You may feel that the best way to revolutionize your child's education is to remove him or her from the public school system altogether and send your child to a private school. In our house, that is the choice we have made. There are people who consider that to be unreasonable because of the cost of private education. There is no doubt that it may cause you to reprioritize your spending, but it is by far one of the greatest investments you will ever make. There is much more value and appreciation in driving a late-model used car while sending your child to a Christ-honoring school than there is in driving a brand-new car while putting the child through the muck and mire of the public educational system. Consider it this way: a new car depreciates the moment you drive it off the lot, but your children will *appreciate* in value when you raise them to honor the Lord.

You might even find a person in your church who is able to home-school a group of children and organize willing families to work together to see that your children are given the opportunity to be taught in a godly manner. Your local church may also consider such a program with the right amount of involvement from the membership. I cannot think of any better mission for a group of church members to work on together than the education of the children in the congregation.

What if like-minded Christian businessmen decided to set aside resources from their companies every year to fund a Christian school in their city with scholarships for deserving children? Consider the impact not only on the lives of the individual recipients but also on the future of the city and generations to come. When a young man or young lady is taught ethics—not from the relative approach of the secular world, but from the biblical approach of right and wrong—you will have a child who will grow up to be a responsible adult. He or she will, in turn, become a leader in the community who will be a blessing not only to family, children, and church but also to those in the community upon whom they have an impact—and even the nation and world. This kind of programming creates a chain reaction of benefit that has a far-reaching impact for years to come.

No matter what approach you take, you need to know that it is going to require a great deal of commitment. It requires *commitment in the home* so that the child sees the biblical principles you want taught in school lived out through your family life. It will need a *financial commitment*, either by being a blessing to a public school teacher or through tuition dollars to a private school, which you have chosen for your child to attend, or through a home school co-op, which will need some type of financial assistance. It will require a *commitment of endurance*; understand this: the circumstances are not going to change overnight. And it will require the *ongoing efforts* of one generation after the next.

Each must be willing and responsible to pick up where the other left off and make a Christian presence felt and objectives known continually.

The revolution our educational system requires is possible, one day at a time, if you are willing to take every inch you can get and not give any ground back. It is a waste of time to act as if we are suffering unjustly when we don't see the reform we wish. Working responsibly to create the difference we need is something that will change the world, one small victory at a time.

Step 4.3: A Small Victory Is Better Than No Victory

- The educational revolution will come one day at a time.

- Every person will be required to do his or her individual part.

- If it doesn't work at your house, don't expect it to work at the schoolhouse.

Questions to Consider

1. What can I do to wage guerrilla warfare on a broken educational system?

   _____

   _____

2. Am I willing to stay committed to the change I want to create?

   _____

   _____

Step 4.4

GET THEM WHILE THEY ARE YOUNG

THE WAY YOU start out doesn't always determine how you'll turn out, but it sure does set the tone. At Cornerstone we like to say, "Everything good starts at church." One Sunday each month we have an opportunity for parents to bring their children before the congregation to be dedicated to the Lord. It is our way of getting them off to a good start. It is important to remember that your children get their start at home. Depending on when they start school, their first five years are yours to mold and shape, so make the most of them.

It has been said, "Whoever owns the family owns the future." I couldn't agree more. There is an all-out culture war being waged for the future of the family, and it is closely connected with schools. Consider the family that has to face life without a father. When those children go to school, they will be looking for leadership to fill the void of the one that should be at home. The young man will turn to a coach or a teacher or gang leader to guide him through what he doesn't want to face alone. A girl will turn to the arms of another man, hoping to find the affirmation she missed from the absentee father.

There are cases where an incomplete or nontraditional family are unavoidable, but that doesn't change the design that God intended to be in place from the very beginning of a child's life and for it to be the foundational unit in their education. God's ideal family is a father and a mother raising their children in the home, preparing them to go into every man's world and be a light shining for God's glory. If you want to know what's going on in the country, look at what's going on in the home, and you will find the answer. If the home is falling apart, the country is falling apart. If the housewife is financially strapped, then the government is strapped. If the children are being neglected in the home, why do we expect their needs to be met at a school? That is why one of the greatest things you can do to revolutionize education is to keep your family together.

This is a lot harder than it used to be. I am thirty-two years old, and I can tell you that when I was a child, there were a great number of people whom you could count on for instruction and guidance. If you happened to live in a home where Mom and Dad were not doing their part, then you would go to school and *Coach Martin* would tell you, "Son, this is right, and this is wrong!" Or you would go to church, and *Sister Smith* would put her arm around you, smiling, and say, "Child, don't you know God thinks you are one of a kind?" I am not saying that people like this do not exist anymore, but they are certainly harder to find. It seems that most children are put in mass-care facilities until they are old enough to get into school, and without any foundation or structure at home, it's too late for them to receive the proper guidance and nurturing they require. There is no doubt that raising children is a challenge, but it's one that, by God's grace, you are given the strength to do.

The schools may have changed during the past thirty years, and society has certainly changed in the last thirty years, but God has not changed, and neither has the blessing of children. We need to look at what has worked, ignore what has not, and reach out to our children while they are young. Ephesians 6:4 says, "Fathers, do not provoke your children to wrath, but bring them up in the training and admonition of the LORD." That process starts early and never stops.

I have heard my father say many times, "God gives each child two parents so that at all times they have one good one." It indeed takes two. The Bible often refers to *fathers,* not to the exclusion of the mother, but due to the fact that on the day you got married you became one, and God sees both of you, or He sees neither of you. When the Bible talks to the fathers, it's talking to fathers and mothers, because they are the representatives of the household. That's why the epidemic of men walking out on the family and putting the extra burden on the mother must stop. If you are looking at walking out on your obligation as a father because you think it's just too hard, you better look again. In Exodus 20:5 the Lord made a very harsh promise: "I, the LORD your God, am a jealous God, visiting the iniquity of the fathers on the children to the third and fourth generations of those who hate Me." When you abandon your children, you abandon your grandchildren and your great-grandchildren. The more frightening reality is what will happen when the abandoned and untaught generation have children.

We are instructed not to provoke our children. Let me begin by taking an opposite approach. If we are not to provoke them, it would stand to reason that our primary function is to encourage them. Anyone who knows me is well aware of my affection for horses. I share the sentiments of Ronald Reagan and Sir Winston Churchill, who said, "When you are on a great horse, you have the best seat you will ever have."[1] There is a rule when training horses that I have applied many times as a father: *make the right things easy and the hard things difficult.* Train through encouragement. When I was a child, I always enjoyed the days when I behaved well, because they were rewarded with encouragement. "I'm proud of you, son." "You are doing a great job." "Keep up the good work." "You're going to make it, my champion!" These were just some of the constantly encouraging phrases that I heard.

Notice I said *the days when*…I was by no means a perfect child, I am unaware of any perfect children who have been born other than the virgin-born Son of God. Every time I required correction, I was not belittled for my actions; they just became the hardest thing in the world to try and do. In other words, over time it was very clear that the rules were the rules, and I was encouraged to follow them. If I did not, I wouldn't get away with it, and life would be much easier and more pleasant for all if I freely chose to obey.

Because of this method of encouragement growing up, I never wondered if I was somebody. I knew that no matter what the world outside said or thought about me, I was somebody at home. I knew loud and clear what Mom and Dad thought about me, and my significance in their eyes meant more than words can say. I didn't need the bad influences at school to tell me I was cool; I knew I was cool when I got off the bus. I wasn't looking for acceptance in a gang; I already had it; Dad was the leader, Momma was the co-captain, and we all had each other's backs. Because of the encouragement they instilled in me at an early age, I do my utmost to do the same with my three young children each and every day.

You can provoke your children through abandonment or through neglect. Neglect can be your absence in their daily lives because you are too busy to give them your attention, which a child desperately needs. You must let your children know every day that there is nothing in your life more important to you than them. The best way to do this is to prioritize them above everything else. Put them ahead of your career, your aspirations and desires, your unfulfilled and unrealized dreams. I think we have all seen sons or daughters who are forced to play a role that was not intended for them so their parents could live vicariously through them. You were not blessed with children to turn them into all you never could be; your role as a parent is to help them become all that they can possibly be.

You can encourage or provoke your children through your behavior. If you yell at your wife, they will yell at her too. If you talk behind your husband's back, they will exhibit the same disloyal behavior. If you behave one way in public and another behind closed doors, don't think your charade will last forever, because your children will snitch on you. I always find it funny when a child comes to church and throws an absolute fit, kicking and screaming and swatting at Mom, and then you get to hear how he never acts like this at home. Get serious; who he is there is who he is here, and what he is waiting for is someone to show him how he should act at all times.

I cannot overemphasize how important it is for you to start as early as possible to make a positive impression on your child's life. Some of you may feel it's not possible due to your work situation or financial circumstances, but I promise you, it will save you time, money, and heartache in the long run. You cannot send a tormented and angry eight-year-old who has been provoked by abandonment or neglect to school and expect to receive a well-mannered angel back at home that afternoon. If you will spend quality time with your family, then you can keep them together. If your children are together, then the school will not be able to pull them apart.

Step 4.4: Get Them While They Are Young

- As goes the family, so goes the future.

- You are to encourage, not provoke, your children.

- Make the right thing easy and the wrong thing hard.

- The investment that you make will pay off in the long run.

Questions to Consider

1. Am I provoking my children by my own behavior, and what can I do to change it?

    _____

    _____

2. What are five ways every day that I can encourage my child?

    _____

    _____

Step 4.5

IMPLEMENT THE REVOLUTIONARY POWER OF THE BLESSING

ONE OF MY favorite verses in the Bible is a declaration that I make on a daily basis: "If God is for us, who can be against us?" (Romans 8:31). These words are a constant reminder to me of the blessing of God, my heavenly Father, in my life. The very thought of this scripture reminds me that the Almighty is on my side, and no matter what I encounter in a day, it can't match or stand up to who He is and what He can do on my behalf. This particular verse reminds me not only of the heavenly Father's blessing but also of my earthly father's blessing and how it revolutionized my life and can do the same for you.

Not only does God consider the father as the representative of the household, but the father is also God's representative to the household. How the children relate to their earthly father will determine how they relate to God. In all the ways in which a father can represent God to his family, none is more important and powerful than through the paternal blessing. The Bible tells us that with the tongue we have the power to speak life or death (Proverbs 18:21). What we say can and will become reality, because our words are packed with punch.

Look at the biblical model for this concept, and you will find that when a father laid his hands upon his children and prayed a prayer of blessing over them, exactly what he said became the reality of their life. Why? Because he had the authority to do so. You are the one who has the authority over the life of your child, not just in the natural sense but in the supernatural as well. Consider Jacob and Esau. Their lifelong fight was over the father's blessing. They seemed to know that there was a point in time when the blessings of God upon their father would transfer into their own lives, and both struggled to be in place to receive it.

The best thing you can do for your children is to put your hands on them and bless them. Pray the promises of God over them. Look up scriptures that you want to see become reality in their futures and declare, based upon God's Word, that these are the promises you are claiming. This has a revolutionary impact on the lives of your children and can turn the schools they attend around as well. The power of the blessing will do more to change your child's outcome than all other forces combined.

Consider some of the things that you find in the Word of God pertaining to the lives of those who are the children of God. There are promises of provision. Just look at the Twenty-Third Psalm. In six short verses you find more blessings than anyone could ever hope to contain. Think of what would happen if, by laying your hands on your children and praying these verses over them, these blessings become a reality in your children's lives and went with them every morning to and from school.

"The Lord is my shepherd"—you may not be able to watch over them every day, but with the prayer of blessing, God can. "I shall not want"—there is no limit to what God can provide. You need it; He has it—favor, protection, wisdom, health, strength, and understanding. All of these are biblically based promises that pertain to God's provision, and they can be a blessing to your children on their campus every day.

The third verse says, "He leads me." There are far too many distractions to list in the environment of education that, if your children were to follow any of these paths, would surely destroy their souls. However, if through prayer you place God in charge of leading them in their paths, then you will have nothing to fear.

Verse 4 declares, "I will fear no evil." Can you think of anything better than to bless your children with such freedom in such a hostile place? I probably like verses 5 and 6 the best when it comes to schools: "You prepare a table before me in the presence of my enemies....Surely goodness and mercy shall follow me all the days of my life." I cannot think of anything better to have on campus with my children than the goodness and mercy of God following them. Should my son or daughter find himself or herself facing an enemy, I know that through the blessings of God He will show up and serve my child at His table Himself. Knowing the power of the father's blessing and having experienced it in my own life, I can tell you there is nothing more beneficial than seeing it become a reality in your everyday existence. There is no way that I will let a day go by without providing the same covering for my children that my father provided for me.

One additional reason why the father's blessing is so revolutionary is because it is such a distinct change from what children are accustomed to hearing. Many children do not live under the blessing of the father but under his curse. Many dads are more apt to say, "Well, that was stupid," or "What are you, dumb?" than to say, "You are a blessing, and you can do all things. Keep trying, son." When you speak such harsh words, even if in jest, you are not blessing your children, but in fact you are accomplishing the exact opposite—you are cursing them. Remember that the tongue has the power of life and death. There is no in-between; you are speaking one or the other.

The power of the blessing is a supernatural stick of dynamite, because it doesn't focus on anything that the child has done but sets the course for what each child will do and become. Parents are accustomed to praising their children for their accomplishments. If they make good grades, we say, "My, you're a genius!" When they score twenty points in a basketball game, we say, "Wow, you're a superstar!" These comments have their place in the relationship, but if that is the only time your child hears positive feedback from you, then that child will start believing you love him or her for what he or she does and not for who they are.

But when you extend your hands and begin to bless your children with the words of your mouth, you are establishing all that God will do in their futures. One of the most inspiring things on Planet Earth for a child to hear is that God has something special in store for that child and every one of his or her tomorrows. With your words you are pouring the fuel into your child that they will need to help push through the hard days. You are letting them know, even though they may face what seems like a setback at one time or another, that the God who never fails is still on His throne and still watching over them, and if they will continue to try, God Himself will see to it that everything will be all right.

If God thought enough about the power of the blessing to affirm His own Son before He faced the world, don't you think it's important enough to affirm yours? If you have tried everything you can think of to impact your children's lives and nothing seems to work, lay your hands on them and bless them and see if things don't turn around.

Step 4.5: Implement the Revolutionary Power of the Blessing

- The tongue has the power of life and death.

- You, as the parent, have supernatural authority over your child's life.

- What you say will come to pass, one way or the other.

Questions to Consider

1. Is the power of the blessing a part of my child's life? If not, why not?

_____

_____

2. What are the blessings of God that I want to see come to pass in my child's life?

    _____

    _____

Step 4.6

IT'S A TUG-OF-WAR, SO PULL HARD!

EVERYONE IS FAMILIAR with the old playground game of tug-of-war. Two groups of people each pick up an end of a rope that is knotted in the middle and then pull in opposite directions in an effort to destabilize the opposition and pull them over the center to the other side. Without a doubt the analogy is a perfect portrait of the problem with education in America today. On one side are the family and the church; on the other are the school and the government. The knot in the middle is your child, and he or she is being stretched to the point of coming apart. The winner of this tug-of-war doesn't see his opponent pulled in the mud; he sees his entire future either won or lost. This game is for keeps, so you have to make up your mind that you are going to pull, and pull hard.

However, while the government and the school are pulling on their end of the rope, most parents refuse to even pick up their end. In order to fully appreciate the picture, you need to take a moment and look at how this apathetic problem progressed over time.

There was a time in America when *homeschooling* was the only option. Children received all their education under the supervision of their parents. If your mom and dad could read and write, they would teach you to read and write. If a trade was all they knew, then they would pass their knowledge and experience on to their children as well. While this did not create the standardization that we have today where every age group of school children can be measured by a basic skills test, it did create the generational transference of a basic principle for making the family stronger, one that is missing in today's world. Many children crave the opportunity to learn from their moms and dads, and far too many are frustrated because they are being ignored.

From the home school came the one-room schoolhouse. As society began to grow and develop, the people of a town would build one building and hire a teacher, and the children of that community would attend the one-room schoolhouse to be taught as a group. Education was essentially *private*, because the resources of each town, village, or city came from the private citizens of their own free will, and those resources supported the education of the children. If, as a member of the community, you opted out of the one-room schoolhouse, you were free to do so.

Today the game is totally different. By law, you as a parent are required to have your child in some form of education. If they are enrolled in a public school and not attending class, the truant officer comes looking for them—or, in some cases, for you. If they are not enrolled in a public school and are being taught in a private setting, the tax collector still comes looking for you. Either way, if you do not participate in the government's centralized educational program, you are breaking the law. With that kind of pressure on the parent, most refuse to engage in the tug-of-war for the education of your child.

What happened? And how did we end up so far away from having direct influence in our children's education? Parents got too busy. They could not give their children the basic educational tools, so they made the government responsible, and the government became the *schoolhouse*. It is evident that now the classroom has the power to mold and shape the future, so now the government is not willing to give the power back to the parents. But I have news for you. That is not for them to decide. You should not have to ask permission to take back what is already yours. The school was originally intended to function as an extension of the home, not in spite of it. You are the provider for the basics in your child's life. It's time to pick up your end of the rope and start pulling.

I am not suggesting that a mom and dad should pick up the textbook and start giving a lecture on fractions, equations, or molecular structures. But I am talking about you, as the parent, taking the time to give your child the basic lessons of life. With a prayer of blessing you can inspire your child. With effort and attention to detail, you can have influence at the school your child attends. But all of the inspiration and influence in the world means very little without the right application. My father has told his congregation time and time again, "Inspiration without application leads to frustration." This could change if the parents in their own homes will get back to the basics of applying the truth for life.

Moses told Israel in Deuteronomy 6:1–2:

> Now this is the commandment, and these are the statutes and judgments which the LORD your God has commanded to teach you, that you may observe them in the land which you are crossing over to possess, that you may fear the LORD your God, to keep all His statutes and His commandments which I command you, you and your son and your grandson, all the days of your life, and that your days may be prolonged.

You may read this scripture and say to yourself, "I know. I've already taught my kids the Ten Commandments. I am sure they can quote them as well as any child." But the real question is, can they live them? Moses wasn't just referring to the top ten on God's list; he was going to teach them God's commandments in all matters of life. Through God's Word Moses would share the *basics* on stewardship of natural and financial resources and domestic policy as to how to govern the nation and the home. From top to bottom God laid the responsibility of preparing your children for the future on your shoulders, so that you, your son, and your grandson might fear the Lord all the days of your life and that your days might be prolonged. There's a promise connected to this educational system that I believe everyone would like to have.

You cannot read God's policy on education and think for a minute that He has it so compartmentalized that you are just responsible for the memory verses and the school is responsible for everything else.

In matters of your family, the buck stops with you. Parents have to stop compartmentalizing the responsibility for their children's welfare if they are going to pull them in the right direction and see their lives take proper paths. Recently I had another parent warn me about a class my daughter was attending. "Don't put her in that class. There's a little boy who throws terrible temper tantrums, and if she goes in there, then she'll come home and do it too, just like my daughter did!"

My response seemed to upset this parent. "She may try it once, but she won't ever do it again. I can help her clearly understand why that is not good behavior and will not be tolerated. Bad kids don't make my kid bad; bad parenting does!" After that parent caught his breath, I explained what I am writing to you now. You are the one responsible to teach the truth and instill knowledge in your child's life.

The parent I was speaking with was so indoctrinated with centralized education that he felt it was the responsibility of the school to make sure his child behaved. It's not. The school has a responsibility to see that your child is not hindered by the bad behavior of others, but if your child misbehaves, that's your fault. The only way to willingly receive this concept is to take personal responsibility for your child, pick up your end of the rope at home, and start pulling.

For every hour that your child spends in a godless environment, he should spend two hours in a God-honoring one. When you do the math on an eight-hour school day, it means you have to be a God-honoring home 24-7, which means more than just the prayer at mealtimes and bedtime. It means more than just getting your children to church for an hour and half on Sunday. It means teaching your children the commandments that they may enjoy prolonged life in the land they are to possess. They will *live* in a God-honoring way by watching you live in a God-honoring way.

Your children can indeed possess, make an impact, and prosper in everyman's world, but you have to be the one to instill the basics. I know that people of faith are making a difference in every field of business and in every scope of society. From business to education, from politics to social work, there are good people doing a great work at every level. However, you must also recognize that this didn't happen by accident.

At some point in those involved parents' lives, someone in each person's life picked up the end of the rope and started to pull. They refused to allow the influences of a broken system to claim another life and cause it to become another statistic. They engaged in the battle and steadily decentralized the opposition enough to drag it over to the other side—the right side that leads to a prolonged life filled with God's blessings. You need to start pulling for your own children. If you don't, someone else will.

Step 4.6: It's a Tug-of-War, So Pull Hard!

- Your child is the knot in the middle of the rope being pulled in two directions.

- Because of the power to shape the future in the class-room, the government does not want to give back the influence it's been given.

- It's not theirs to take; it's yours to keep.

Questions to Consider

1. Am I pulling for my children as hard as I should?

_____

_____

2. What can my child tell others that he or she has learned from me?

_____

_____

Step 4.7

REFUSE TO BE FENCED IN

I AM HOPEFUL THAT by now you have started to grasp you indeed have some say-so, some power and authority in the realm of education. Many people feel that because of their circumstances and our political system, they have no option in the matter. The truth is that they have allowed themselves to be fenced in. Let me further illustrate with this analogy.

When I was a young boy, my father owned a hog farm southeast of San Antonio. It was more than just an agricultural endeavor; it was a pork-producing machine. It kept the five mouths of his young children fed and produced a supplement to his income that, for many years, was the difference between staying ahead or falling behind. He sold the old farm years ago, but what a bill of sale can never erase are the memories that you make at a place; those you own forever.

One of the pests you have to manage in an operation like this one is wild pigs. They can devastate your breeding program and cause multiple problems, both in the health and welfare of the herd, not to mention the impact it would have on the bottom line. I bring this topic up not to give you an insight on hog farming but to illustrate a surefire way to catch them every time: *offer them free food, and lots of it.*

Wild pigs are always in search of something to eat. The way you fence them in is to begin placing large amounts of feed in a certain area and then wait until the younger piglets get accustomed to eating it. Not long after the young ones do it, the big pigs follow. When they get acclimated to finding food in that location every day, then you can build one side of what will eventually be a four-sided fence. After a few more days, when they have gotten used to one fence, you can build another, and then another, and finally, when all four sides are up and they are still coming to the free food, all that's left to do is close the gate, and they are yours.

They are still on the same dirt where they used to roam freely. They have not left the farm, but they are now confined to this one area where you can control them, and their freedom is gone for good. The point should be pretty clear: by taking the *free* benefits the government is willing to provide, we find ourselves being fenced in. We are still living in the land of the free and home of the brave; we just have less opportunity to move around as we choose. Now, more than ever before, we must pay close attention to the fences that are being built around us and either demand they be removed or stop eating the free food.

You must remember who you are, not only as a member of the body of Christ but also as a citizen of the United States. You must refuse to allow the government to build a fence around you because of your beliefs. The government of the United States was established by people of faith for the purpose of having a nation that practiced freedom of religion, not freedom *from* religion. In recent years we have forgotten this basic principle and have instead allowed history, in many ways, to be rewritten.

Regarding freedom of religion, I do not have the power to force my religion on you, and you cannot force yours on me. For example, I cannot make it a punishable crime for someone not to go to church on Sunday just because my faith adheres to the practice. The fence that the government has erected through free education is the freedom from religion, where there is no God at all. The government has legislated schools to the point that a child who privately practices his or her faith is being persecuted on his or her own school campus for his or her beliefs.

We, the people of faith in this country, are being fenced out of the arena of education based on a gross misinterpretation and bad implementation of our founding principles. Schools have excluded faith from the conversation, and it is not invited to the table. The confinement of faith to the home and the church are the order of the day. We are as much a part of society as every other person is, and we should have equal opportunity and access and be allowed to discuss our faith openly and unashamedly.

I am not saying that schools should push any kind of religion, but I am saying they should not push out our faith and allow another one in. If they are going to teach alternative lifestyles, then let the Christian alternative be mentioned. If they are going to propose sex education and proper use of a condom, then let the Christian perspective of abstinence and no sex outside of the relationship of marriage be taught also. If you are going to inform children about the ills of substance abuse, then don't hesitate to teach the concept of how sobriety and problem solving through faith fit in. If, in the area of science, we are going to learn the *theory* of evolution, then let me represent the *theory* of Creation to the same class and allow them the freedom to decide.

People, we are being fenced in! We have convinced ourselves that we have no legal place in the field of education. That is not so, and we are responsible to change it! A revolution in the way our children are being taught is required. If we don't make a difference in the classroom, then children in the classrooms will revolt. But if we each take the responsibility that we have, we then can turn things around for our children, their children, and generations to come.

Section 4 Review: Seven Lessons That Will Change the Future of Education

4.1. Stop outsourcing your authority.

4.2. Take control of the campus.

4.3. Small victories are better than no victories at all.

4.4. Get them while they are young.

4.5. Implement the revolutionary power of the blessing.

4.6 It's a tug-of-war, so pull hard.

4.7 Refuse to be fenced in.

Question to Consider

1. Write out ten things you can do to make a difference in the education of your children or grandchildren.

_____

_____

_____

Section Five

POLITICAL
RESPONSE-ABILITY

Seven Lessons to Make a Political Difference

A S A STUDENT of history, I have often read historical accounts and pictured familiar faces of family and loved ones playing a role in the drama that unfolded in the past. For some reason, when I read about our Founding Fathers, I always pictured the face of my grandfather throwing tea into the Boston Harbor, kneeling in prayer at the first meeting of the Continental Congress, or standing up and declaring a hardy *amen* as Patrick Henry announced, "Give me liberty or give me death." I assure you, I did this for two reasons: One, I saw my grandfather as a founding figure in the family, and it was easy to associate him with the birth of a nation. Two, like Henry of old, my grandfather was geared for conflict.

Many felt that Henry was so up for a fight that if there wasn't one going on at the time, he would simply start it. I do not view him in this light but rather as a person with the courage to confront what he wanted to change. My personal favorite quote of Patrick Henry's is this: "I have but one lamp by which my feet are guided; and that is the lamp of experience. I know of no way judging the future but by the past."[1] My grandfather's favorite Bible quote was, "Your word I have hidden in my heart, that I might not sin against You!" (Psalm 119:11). He, like Mr. Henry, felt the quality of one's life and the future were determined by the resources one depended on.

If you use history as a resource, you'll find patterns of predictability that cannot be denied. If you use the Bible as a resource, then you will find these truths: "Blessed is the nation whose God is the LORD" (Psalm 33:12). "Righteousness exalts a nation, but sin is a reproach to any people" (Proverbs 14:34). "When the righteous are in authority, the people rejoice" (Proverbs 29:2). Putting these three verses together, you will conclude that the historical cycles recorded in the Scriptures and in the short history of our very own nation are absolute truth.

When the nation of Israel had its relationship with God in proper order and the Israelites were living the right way, they were blessed. When they sought to live according to His Word and commandments, the nations of the world came to see the wonders that God brought to Israel and to exalt them above other nations. Every time there was a king, leader, or judge who did what was right in the eyes of the Lord, the people he was in authority over were blessed. When the people were blessed because of the righteous acts of their leadership, they rejoiced and celebrated the blessings that flowed into their own lives.

Here in the United States, there was a time when we were the fastest-growing economy in the world and the envy of all other nations. We had every reason to fail and still seemed to succeed. Our vision was so great it changed the destiny of mankind and the history of the world. The combination of equality and freedom created a *shining city on a hill*, and the nation between our borders was called *the land of opportunity*.

Deuteronomy 32:7 says:

> Remember the days of old,
> Consider the years of many generations.
> Ask your father, and he will show you;
> Your elders, and they will tell you.

However, I do not know what our nation and this government are based on from what I see today. I know what it was based on from what my grandparents have told me. As a student of history, I am able to glean from the foundations the past provides and obtain wisdom from others' experiences. The history of this nation clearly reveals that there was to be a mixture of God and government, faith and social freedom. The mandate on this nation was not to create a world ruled solely by religion, or the opposite extreme, ruled by humanistic anarchy, which simply serves the purpose of greed-driven men.

When you read the personal writings of the men who founded this nation—the ones who actually fought in a real revolution, who were responsible to make a difference in their generation that we hope to see in ours—you find people who firmly believed that they lived both in service to God and man, not one or the other. Driven by a sense of destiny and providence and aware of the shortcomings of human nature, they wrote two documents. One, the Declaration of Independence, established that it is God's will that all men whom He created be considered equal. The nature of this document, in many ways, points to what is the divine origin of this nation. The principles set forth in the second document were written with the intention of keeping men from ruling too harshly over one another so that each could live freely before the God who created them. It is called the Constitution of the United States. These two works were brilliantly birthed to serve as aids to one another and to the men who pledged to uphold them and serve others through them. That's history.

Today, in many ways, the amendments of the Constitution are being interpreted by those who were not there and who did not fight, by those who do not see themselves as serving God in heaven by helping their fellow man here on earth but rather are seeking to control other men in an effort to have their own will be done above all others. Instead of having two forces working together for the greater good, the current practice is to use one document, the Constitution, to hinder the other document, the Declaration of Independence, and to force the will of the government on the people. This would be enough to cause the Founding Fathers to roll over in their hallowed graves. I know it would cause my grandfather to do so in his.

When state after state votes that it doesn't wish to recognize homosexual marriage, and then federally appointed judges rule that it is *unconstitutional* not to recognize homosexual marriage, are we upholding the will of the people, or are we telling them what they will do? This is just one of many examples that illustrate how far we have come from where we started. But by taking the right steps we can get back to where we have been.

Too often the debate and banter about excessive religion and liberal secularism in society are lost in the shouting matches of political strife. This section is not devoted to adding to the noise but to sharing seven lessons that will put our faith into action. The topic of faith and freedom, God and government, is a complex one, but by taking simple steps we can establish the following. While you may not believe as I believe, and you may not obey what I obey, you cannot force me to change, and I can only pray that you will see enough virtue in me to follow my example.

In a sermon preached at the Christ Church in Philadelphia on Friday, June 23, 1775, the day George Washington left the city to take command of the Continental Army, Reverend William Smith said, "Religion and liberty must flourish or fall together in America. We pray they both may be perpetual."[2] To those words I say *amen*.

It's time to be politically response-able.

Step 5.1

A NEW KIND OF PARTY

THIS LAST PRESIDENTIAL election left me feeling a bit confused. I am fairly familiar with the common definitions used to describe the different roles played in politics. Elected officials, for example, are called *representatives*. This word is used because by obtaining the majority of the votes in his or her given area of the country, each is elected to *represent* the beliefs, views, and convictions of those who sent them to *serve* his or her term in office.

My confusion in the last election was not based on a term that I was unfamiliar with but on an emotion, which, for the very first time, was very real concerning my representation. I was perplexed because while there were candidates to vote for, I couldn't find one who I felt truly represented me. There were some who might have sounded more like me than others or appeared to be more like me than some, but with a little bit of digging I came to the conclusion I truly had no representative.

There was no one who, without apology, stood for the right to life. Many said they were 95 percent pro-life, but no one said that without a doubt a child is a living being at conception and has the right to live, and that to infringe upon that right is to infringe upon its freedom, because the practice of abortion is murder. Well, of course they aren't going to say that, because if they did, they wouldn't get elected, and I guess that's the problem. They are more interested in the election than they are in representation of the people. They will say what needs to be said in order to get where they want to go and, upon arrival, do as they wish to do.

"Oh, well, Brother Hagee, it's complicated!" Maybe it is for you, but it's pretty clear to me. As a man of God who lives his life in submission to the Bible and considers its words to be absolute literal truth,

I do not feel that I have a representative who clearly represents me in the government today. There are many with whom I agree on certain things, but I am not aware of any about whom I can say they represent me on everything. Keep in mind regarding this representation that I am not speaking as an individual but as a born-again, Bible-believing Christian. When I say *I have no representative*, I am saying that as a Christian I cannot say that I am a Republican and would vote for someone from that party because of my core beliefs, nor am I a Democrat and would vote for someone from that party for the same reason.

I believe the time has come in America to consider a new kind of party—the kind that I can honestly say fully represents me. As citizens, we are entitled to equal representation under the law. Why not pursue what has been purchased by the sacrifice of so many others? Before you write me off as crazy, listen to the kind of party that I am proposing before you determine this will never work.

Remember, I wrote about the economic trends that are traceable through history and that enable us to determine what will happen next. Well, the same is true about politics. There are trends that are so established they have people predicting what will happen politically for the next two decades. They analyze what is known as *indicators* like the unemployment rate and the economy. They look at regions in terms of background and commerce, and they add it all up to tell you who will vote for what in which area of the country. This has gotten so frighteningly predictable that in some cases based on the car I drive and where I live, work, and go to church, you would say, "Well, I know who he is going to vote for."

This needs to stop. In the same way that I suggest we decentralize schools through individual concerted efforts reaching toward the same purpose, I think we should decentralize political parties by letting them know they cannot have our vote until they earn it. Many times either party will count on your vote simply based on the patterns of religious, economical, or cultural stereotypes.

Politicians go into a race saying things like: "Well, I already have the Christian vote…the Hispanic vote…the middle-class vote." Who said they owned it, and what keeps you from changing it? The time has come to clearly establish that if someone wants to *serve* in office, that person had better earn the privilege to do so. Politicians were not born or appointed as royalty, and it is time to remove many of them from their self-appointed thrones. The clearest way to do this is to hold them accountable. If they have earned your vote by the campaign promises they made, keep track of what they said and what they did, and if the two don't match up, don't vote for them again. Decentralize their assumption about who you are and what you will do. Refuse to become a statistic to be captured, and maintain the position of a citizen to be served. Call them, take the time to write them, or even go see them and let them know that you are tracking their representation of you.

If you were an employer and had an employee who said one thing and did another, that person would not work for you very long at all. Why shouldn't the same rule apply when it comes to politics? It is neither my purpose nor my intent to try and tell how you should or for whom you should vote. I am just telling you to vote, and always vote *for you.* Your vote is your voice, and if you don't speak up, you have no right to complain about what you get. Speak up, and tell the complacent career politicians whose gross assumption is that they know what's best for you that they better get busy representing who you are or plan on looking for another line of work.

I know what you are thinking: What if there is no one to vote for? Believe me, I know how you feel, and the truth is, there may not be a nominated candidate for you to vote for, but that doesn't mean that you can't write one in. Think of the impact it would make if millions of Christians all over the country went to the voting booths this next election and let their voices be heard by writing in the name of their pastor as their representative. OK, so now you think I really am crazy, and you are arguing as you read, "Come on, where would that get us? We have to elect someone!"

My response: Did you elect the last one? Would writing in the name of someone you trust to fully represent you make the situation any worse than it is right now? No; as a matter of fact, I think it would have made it better. It may not change the outcome, but it would cause all of those people who like to follow the trends and determine how you vote by what you drive, the color of your skin, and where you worship to say, "There's a new kind of party starting to form." Not a party centered on color or denomination or salary, but a party that is not pleased with those who are running for office and is looking for an alternative. What would the Republicans and Democrats be doing if they saw that in the last election they lost millions of votes, which they had assumed were going to be theirs? Do you think it would be business as usual, or do you think they would be looking for a way to win your confidence back?

Any time you sign a financial document concerning who is going to pay for what in the agreement, you see these words: *responsible party.* I think that would be a great name for the new kind of party I propose: *the Responsible Party.* After all, we are the ones financially responsible for the consequences of the choices being made, and we are the ones who are socially responsible for the quality of life in the cities and states where our children are being raised, and we are the ones spiritually responsible for seeing the blessings of God brought back to this nation again. Let the Responsible Party raise its voice, and let those who live in a fog of blind assumption hear loud and clear that there's a turnaround in this nation's future.

Step 5.1: A New Kind of Party

- You are responsible to choose your representation.

- You are a voice and a vote—not a statistic to be captured and forever retained.

- It's time to get the politicians' attention, because for too long you've been ignored.

Questions to Consider

1. Am I pleased with my representation in the government?

   _____

   _____

2. Am I willing not only to talk outside the political box but also to take action outside the political box?

   _____

   _____

Step 5.2

THE HIGHEST FORM OF GOVERNMENT

THE ONE RESOUNDING theme throughout each section of this book is the role that you as an individual play in the world you desire to change. You cannot change the nation's leaders unless you change the society that elected those leaders. You cannot change the society that elected those leaders unless you change the environment in which they were educated. You cannot change the educational environment unless you change the economic one. You cannot change the economy unless you change the church, and you cannot change the church until you are willing to change the people in the church—*which brings us to you*. When we talk about government, I think that it is truly important to understand how it starts and where it is the most potent. Self-governance is the highest form of government.

I have heard many people argue that if the Founding Fathers of this nation were Christian in their beliefs, why didn't they establish a national Christian church, which would have settled it? Nothing could be further from the truth—they had just separated themselves from a government that had a nationalized church. That was one of the reasons why people began to migrate to this country to begin with. The other reason, and probably the more powerful one, is this: Why would they mandate forced obedience to religious rule when the very author and finisher of the faith doesn't mandate it of His own creation? God Himself gives every man the opportunity to choose. For certain, every choice has its consequence, whether good or bad, but you choose the end result; no one else can. This right of choice is what is known as *volition*, and every man has it. It is how you use it that determines how well you govern yourself.

Before we get impassioned about holding the government or our elected officials or even our schools and churches accountable for where we are, we first need to ask ourselves if we are willing to hold ourselves accountable for where we are. In the end, that is how God will judge you—based on you and no one else. It won't be based on your background or political history, nor on the society you live in or your surroundings, but on how you handled yourself under the guidance of His law. "So then each of us shall give account of himself to God" (Romans 14:12). If you hold the answer to the outcome, then you are the highest form of government, and that is called *self-government*. If you want to live a life the way it is intended to be lived...if you want to maintain your freedom and not live hindered by any type of dictator...then you will need to have a proper respect for self-government. If you don't properly govern yourself, then nothing else in your world will work. As the Bible states, "First remove the plank from your own eye, and then you will see clearly to remove the speck out of your brother's eye" (Matthew 7:5).

It is from a position of self-governing that you can get involved in other forms of government. Time and again I have heard people say, "Well, I would run for office, but it's a dirty business, and that's why I can't get involved." That would be the same as saying, "My baby's diaper is dirty, and that's why I can't change it." Wrong! If you know it needs to be changed, have enough self-rule to do what needs to be done.

My wife and I have been blessed with three beautiful children. Because the typical family in America today normally has just two, one of each and that's it, we often get asked, as if we were wild-eyed radicals, "How many more are you going to have?"

We have a very standard and gracious answer: "We will see what God allows."

Then there is the typical follow-up question: "Well, aren't you worried about having more children because of the things that are going on in the world today?"

The answer to that question is a lot shorter and much easier to understand; in multiple languages, "NO!" I can't find a place in the Bible where God says, "Be fruitful and multiply as long as things in the world are calm, your taxes are low, and your political party is in office." He simply gave the command to be fruitful and multiply. Let me ask you this question: What would happen to the world if, in the future, all the *good* people quit having babies? I am not saying that my wife and I are better than anyone else. What I am saying is that when people use the logic that the world is too rough to live in right now, I don't start looking for another world; I do what I can to change the world I am in, which requires the daily discipline of living a life of self-governance.

The greatest decision you can make regarding the governing of your life is to subject yourself—heart, soul, mind, and body—to the authority of God. Every person who is response-able no matter what occurs in the world around him lives this way. It is a choice that no government can make for you or school can impress upon you. This one decision, regardless of the world you are living in, will start you on the road of your revolution, and that is when you'll begin making a difference.

Step 5.2: Self-Government Is the Highest Form of Government

- You will have to give an answer for you.

- Volition is the freedom to choose.

- Choose to subject yourself to the authority of God.

Questions to Consider

1. Do I hold myself accountable for my actions as much as I hold others accountable for theirs?

_____

_____

2. Am I willing to change the world that I am in by governing myself, or do I allow the government of the world to change me?

_____

_____

Step 5.3

YOU ARE WHAT HE IS LOOKING FOR

W HEN GEORGE WASHINGTON was commissioned to lead the Continental Army, he went in search of willing and able men who wanted to join the cause. The God of heaven is very much the same. He is not the leader of an army that fights with weapons of destruction that harm lives, but He is the leader of an army that combats destruction with the kind of revolutionary love that will change lives. With that being said, the God of heaven may be looking for you to join the fight in the political realm. If you have submitted your life to Him and are governing your life according to His Word, then you may be exactly what He needs. "Well, which political ticket would I be on?" His ticket! Christians who live by the Word of God should be believers governed by the Word before they are categorized and held to the substandard platform of any political party. You may be Republican, Democrat, or Independent, but your faith should supersede all of those things when it comes to governing your life.

Sometimes people say, "Well, I just don't know how the Bible and politics mix."

First, let me say the Bible is full of politics; it has been, is, and will always be. Look at the New Testament. The church and government were in almost every line. John the Baptist pointed out the immoral conduct of Herod and was executed for it (Mark 6:14–29). Paul and his traveling companions were charged with treason for making the claim: "There is another king, Jesus" (Acts 17:7). Or, if you think it is outdated, consider what is to come. Revelation 13:1–10 speaks of an entire coalition in which the Antichrist is the leader of a centralized government on Earth, and he will lead the earth to direct rebellion against God. He (the Antichrist) will set up his political system of pure evil. Like it or not, the Bible is full of political affairs, so there goes that excuse.

The second thing I often hear people say is, "Well, I am not sure that God wants to use me."

Sure He does. Look at Isaiah 6:8:

> I heard the voice of the LORD, saying: "Whom shall I send, and who will go for Us?" Then I said, "Here am I! Send me."

These are the words of Isaiah as he was commissioned to do the work of the Lord. It is easy to see that God is clearly searching for people to do the work—which means He needs you.

The final thing people use to be complacent is the old "Well, the end is already written, so there's not much we can change anyhow."

God is sovereign, and His will shall be done. Don't you think it's better to be a part of His plan than simply to sit back and watch it unfold? Throughout the Bible you see God strategically place His people in positions of political influence in order to accomplish what He desired. Joseph served in the highest office, second to Pharaoh in Egypt. Daniel was a government official in Babylon and Persia, both pagan cultures that did not live according to his system of belief. Nehemiah and Esther had significant political roles to play, and it was for the purpose of carrying out the plan of a sovereign God.

Politically, God is active in every chapter of world history, whether you have knowledge of it or not. Don't you think that if He is politically active, maybe then you should be too?

Faith and politics do indeed mix, but how? Christ answered it in Matthew 22:15–21. His religious and political enemies tried to team up and trap Him with His own words. They asked Him a trick question on the separation of church and state. They thought Christ would be forced to take one side or the other and in doing so would give them the chance to either disqualify His claim of Messiah or get Him in real trouble with the law. Here was the question, and it is still being asked by some today: "Is it lawful to pay taxes to Caesar, or not?" (verse 17). With those words you could see these pious twerps smirk with the expression of *gotcha* on their faces. If Christ said it was unlawful, then He would be condemned for treason. If He said it was lawful, He would be siding with a foreign government and oppressing His own people, which meant He could not be the one who was anointed to deliver them. Either way the trap was set.

As I said earlier, there are many who still ask this question today, and the answer Christ gave then is still the same. It establishes how politics and faith mix. "But Jesus perceived their wickedness, and said, 'Why do you test Me, you hypocrites? Show Me the tax money.' So they brought Him a denarius" (verses 18–19).

I can almost see the confusion on their faces, "Where in the world is He going with this one?" When they brought the coin to Jesus, He looked at it and asked them a question: "Whose image and inscription is this?" (verse 20).

In order to not seem foolish they said, "Caesar's!"

So then, with Caesar's coin in His hand, Christ responded to their question: "Render therefore to Caesar the things that are Caesar's, and to God the things that are God's" (verse 21). The message: The money you have in your coin purse has the face of a political figure on it; therefore it doesn't belong to God. By taking the money and using it for your own purposes, then you have accepted its authority, and if you accept its authority, then give what is owed back. If you accept God's authority and live by His resources, then give God what He is owed, which is your life in service to Him and others.

Remember that the Founding Fathers of this nation thought they were people like Joseph, Daniel, Nehemiah, and Isaiah: men who were willing to be a part of God's plan at God's time for their generation and those to come. They were people who were willing to refuse the things that came from those who sought to oppress them in order to live under the authority of Him who makes men free. Had they not been willing to get involved, had they not been willing to be used, had they thought the end was already written, so what good will it do anyway, then who knows where we'd be today.

What I do know is that God was looking for men like them to help revolutionize their generation, and He may be looking for a response-able person like you to help revolutionize this one.

"Whom shall I send?"

"Here I am, send me."

Step 5.3: You Are What He's Looking For

- The Bible and politics have always been intertwined.

- God is the Sovereign and His will shall be done, but He wants to include you.

- He places people strategically where He needs them, when He needs them, to accomplish His plan.

Questions to Consider

1. What are my personal hindrances to becoming more politically involved?

_____

_____

2. Am I willing to get over these hindrances so God can use me to turn things around?

_____

_____

Step 5.4

THE POLITICAL ACTION
OF THE KINGDOM

EVERY YEAR SINCE I can remember, my father has been approached with offers to have the church become politically involved. Sometimes the ideas have been outrageous and at other times truly for a worthy cause, but they have never been acted upon because, as the leader of a body of believers, Pastor Hagee is not commissioned to use his congregation for a political cause. He is ordained to minister to their needs and provide them with inspiration so they can then minister to others. With that said, the question then arises: What are proper, biblically based, political actions? The answer may or may not surprise you.

Proper, biblical, political actions will recognize that God is the ruler over all and take steps to bring our lives back in line with His will. This is not to be accomplished through the process of political upheaval, which would be a change from the top down, but through personal transformation, which leads to political transformation and change from the bottom up.

Do you know the greatest thing I can do as a pastor to impact politics? Preach the salvation message of the cross and share the hope of God's amazing grace. Why not march in the street or picket and protest? Because as a pastor I can share the redemptive power of Jesus Christ, and by so doing, I have been a part of an action that creates a better citizen than any government plan can provide.

But what do we do when the government acts in an unrighteous manner? We do not overthrow; we transform. By the actions of our government, it is apparent that there is no shortage of transformation that needs to be made. This is best accomplished by getting in a position to defend the innocent from the wicked choices of an evil government. Look at Abraham when he heard the judgment that would be unleashed on Sodom and Gomorrah. He placed himself in a position to plead with God to spare the righteous people who were in the city (Genesis 18:16–33). Moses did the same when God was angered by the rebellious actions of the children of Israel as they danced around the golden calf. As God began to consume them, Moses got between the people and God, and the Lord changed His mind (Exodus 32:1–14). There's Esther before Xerxes, begging for her people be spared, and many other instances that establish how we, the community of faith, are to take action concerning political policies we want to see changed.

A very familiar verse is in 2 Chronicles 7:14:

> If My people who are called by My name will humble themselves, and pray and seek My face, and turn from their wicked ways, then I will hear from heaven, and will forgive their sin and heal their land.

The quality of this country, while directly connected to the position of the government, is not contingent upon the government but upon the action the people of God are willing to take. I know that might seem heavy, but as I said, politics and religion can be a very complicated mix.

As Christians, we are commissioned to be watchmen. We are called to keep a watchful eye and go into action whenever evil raises its ugly head to threaten the well-being of our society. The major problem at the moment is that many of God's watchmen are standing at their post with their eyes closed. We should be vigilant in our task of standing between the innocent people of our nation and the wrath of God that is to come. I know it is not a popular thought in modern religion to think about God's wrath, but if He judged Sodom and Gomorrah and then failed to judge this country, He would have to apologize for not being just. We should be like Abraham and plead with God to spare those who are not guilty.

The model of prayer we find from the Lord even demonstrates this type of biblical political action: "And do not lead us into temptation, but deliver us from the evil one. For Yours is the kingdom and the power and the glory forever" (Matthew 6:13). Every ounce of those powerful words brings us back under God's authority and leadership. If we, as the people of God, stay on the political sidelines, how will we know when and where to get involved? It was from her role as queen that Esther was able to influence the king to reverse the order to kill the Jews. Think of what a transformation would take place if a political leader was campaigning to raise prayer support instead of financial support, traveling around the country to stay in touch with people by telling them what was really going on in politics and keeping Christians informed as to how to pray and what to pray for.

Oh, I know you think it would never happen. It has before. Remember the words of Patrick Henry that he looked at the past to guide his future? When the first session of the Continental Congress met, they decided before doing anything else that they should cry out to God in prayer, because the choices they were going to make would certainly impact the lives of other men. When the Civil War raged and the Union was facing destruction, President Abraham Lincoln called for a national day of fasting and prayer—a time for Americans to repent of the sin of slavery and for God to heal us of the crimes that had separated us from other men.

OK, so that was way back when; what about now? In the first week of June 1944, my father was a boy in East Texas who was attending a Bible conference in Waxahachie with his parents. Suddenly, in the middle of the night, a loud knock came to the door of the room where they were sleeping, and the voice on the other side shouted, "The invasion of Europe has begun; everyone to the chapel. We must pray!" My grandparents got up and got dressed and took their children, in the middle of night, to hit their knees and ask the Lord to spare the young men in their small country church who were certainly in harm's way thousands of miles away. Other people in the room called out the names of loved ones; mothers cried for sons, wives for husbands, children for fathers, because while they were enlisted to fight against the horror of the Nazi regime, they were innocent of being a part of the reasons why this battle had started.

They were not the only ones praying. Days earlier, knowing the invasion was scheduled to begin, President Franklin Roosevelt left the White House to go to a familiar place of rest and retreat so he could clearly think of what he wanted to say to the nation. He knew the loss of life in the invasion was going to be great. He knew the American people were going suffer the heartache of thousands of memorial services attended by widows and fatherless children in the days and weeks to come. His purpose for leaving the White House was not as a means of escape, but it was to find the words he needed to encourage a brokenhearted nation after having paid such a tremendous price to liberate the world and maintain liberty.

After the start of his address to the nation on Tuesday evening, June 6, 1944, President Roosevelt said these words: "Almighty God." No matter your religious conviction or political position, there was no doubt that prayer was the only thing to do after the launch of a military operation that would cost more than twenty thousand lives. Following those opening words, there were six minutes of eloquence that came from the heavy heart of a burdened leader who was searching for solace for his people. President Roosevelt continued with the following words:

> Our sons, pride of our Nation, this day have set upon a mighty endeavor, a struggle to preserve our Republic, our religion, and our civilization, and to set free a suffering humanity.
>
> Lead them straight and true; give strength to their arms, stoutness to their hearts, steadfastness in their faith.
>
> They will need Thy blessings. Their road will be long and hard. For the enemy is strong. He may hurl back our forces. Success

may not come with rushing speed, but we shall return again and again; and we know that by Thy grace, and by the righteousness of our cause, our sons will triumph.

They will be sore tired, by night and by day, without rest—until the victory is won. The darkness will be rent by noise and flame. Men's souls will be shaken with the violences of war.

For these men are lately drawn from the ways of peace. They fight not for the lust of conquest. They fight to end conquest. They fight to liberate. They fight to let justice arise, and tolerance and goodwill among all Thy people. They yearn but for the end of the battle, for their return to the haven of home.

Some will never return. Embrace these, Father, and receive them, Thy heroic servants into Thy kingdom....

With Thy blessing, we shall prevail over the unholy forces of our enemy. Help us to conquer the apostles of greed and racial arrogances. Lead us to the saving of our country, and with our sister nations into the world unity that will spell our sure peace—a peace invulnerable to the schemings of unworthy men. And a peace that will let all men live in freedom, reaping the just rewards of their honest toil. Thy will be done, Almighty God. Amen.[1]

The newspapers around the country carried the printed prayer with a written request from the president that the audience read it along with him. If the estimated number is accurate, then more than one hundred million Americans were listening on that Tuesday night in June, and President Roosevelt would lead what had to have been the single largest mass prayer in all of history.

Whether it was the leader of the free world over the radio or the families lying prostrate on the floor of the gymnasium at a Bible school in central Texas, people all over the country were taking political action the night of the invasion, getting in a position to place themselves between the wrath of war and the brave men who were defending freedom.

I know there are some who feel that real political action means doing something terribly brash and offensive in order to attract attention to a cause. Burn a flag. Make a crude poster. Shout insults. Holler chants. Most of the time these actions don't create change; they simply fuel flames of rage and ignite hate. Real political action is the kind that transforms things. If you wish to truly create change through political action, let the change be built upon the foundation and power of intercession and prayer.

Step 5.4: Political Action of the Kingdom

- We are not here to overthrow from the top down; we are here to transform from the bottom up.

- We are watchmen standing at our post to be a force against evil.

- Our force is not comprised of weapons that cause destruction but those that instill hope and rebuild lives.

Questions to Consider

1. When is the last time I took political action for my nation through prayer?

_____

_____

2. What are evils that I see in the government at this time that I can take action against?

_____

_____

Step 5.5

A HOUSE DIVIDED

THE BOOK OF Matthew lays out a principle that certainly applies as fair warning to the nation we live in today. "Every kingdom divided against itself is brought to desolation, and every city or house divided against itself will not stand" (Matthew 12:25). Without a doubt, America is a house divided and has been for some time. *Unity* is a word that is often thrown around but very seldom found. Earlier in this work I described the power of agreement. In that chapter I wrote that we didn't all have to be exactly alike in order to walk in agreement and unity. A major problem in America is that Americans seldom agree on anything. The Left doesn't agree with the Right. The North still doesn't agree in many ways with the South. One culture has its concerns and differences with another and passes it off with cute lines and quips that remind us we are not all alike.

Even more devastating than the fact that the house of Congress is divided is that the house of faith is divided as well. Truthfully, righteousness and unrighteousness—good and evil, light and darkness—are in a race to see who can come together first. Once there is agreement on one side or the other, the battle for the soul of this nation will be won by those who are willing to work together first. The sad news is that the other side is way out in front of the good guys. We have used our faith, interpretation, and traditions to create walls of separation, which enable the divide-and-conquer approach to work rather well. The time has come to get our act together and remind ourselves of what is truly important for the future of our children, our nation, and the world.

Faith in the God of peace, hope, and love should be a unifying factor—not a dividing one. It should be the place where all other differences fade in the light of who He is and what He has done for us.

However, there is a group of people we are not to be unified with according to Scripture, and that line is very clearly defined.

> Blessed is the man
> Who walks not in the counsel of the ungodly,
> Nor stands in the path of sinners,
> Nor sits in the seat of the scornful.
>
> —PSALM 1:1

When it comes to everyone else, by all means do what you can to live in agreement with one another. You don't have to see things exactly the same way, but if you both desire the same result, why not work together to accomplish it? If both Catholic and Protestant desire to see an America without abortion, why not come into agreement on the matter, make a plan, and create a turnaround? Is it because one has *mass*, and another, *service*? How many more lives will be lost in an abortion mill while that all-important debate is discussed?

If Christian and Jew both wish to see the world free of a nuclear Iran, why not set aside differences to see that a worthy goal is reached? "Well, it's more complicated than that." It is if you make the major things minor and the minor things major, and only if you allow past offenses to hinder future progress and if you keep to traditions that relate as much to faith and relationship with God as Tarzan relates to a Rhodes scholar.

By agreeing about matters that are important to people of faith, we can, together, make great political strides toward the turnaround this nation so desperately needs. America is not a church, but it is indeed filled with churches. The time has come for people of faith to speak to one another and stop shouting at each other. We may at times argue, but we should never fight and brawl. There is indeed much we can do if we will walk in agreement, but if we remain divided, we may at best hope to only creep and crawl.

We may not always get it right, but the beauty of our faith is that through accountability, grace, and forgiveness, we can always try again.

Look at the work of the Founding Fathers. They indeed missed the mark on the topic of slavery, but they hit the bull's-eye in many other areas. They sought a religion free from the government, but not a government free from religion. John Adams wrote in a letter to Abigail, his wife, with advice for his sons: "Let them revere nothing but Religion, Morality and Liberty."[1] These were words that benefit the America of the new millennium as much as they did his sons in his day.

When you begin to discuss the notion of interfaith work, mainly of Protestant, Evangelical, and Jew, pseudo-intellectuals and historical revisionists like to argue that the Founding Fathers were drafting documents that were indicative of the nation in their generation and time. The position suggests that they had no clue how pluralistic America would become; after all, they lived in a country where religious diversity was mostly within the realm of Protestantism. While they may not have had the obscene amount of differences we see in our culture today, they were more diverse than you may think. George Washington stated: "The bosom of America is open to receive…the oppressed and persecuted of all Nations and Religions; whom we shall welcome to a participation of all our rights and previleges [sic]."[2] "They may be Mohometans, Jews, or Christians of any Sect, or they may be Atheists."[3] The point is that the Founding Fathers fully expected their system to be tested, and they fully believed that America would pass the test.

The matter is still at hand and is up to us. We are the ones who will determine if the work of those who have come before us will live on or if life in this nation will be so rewritten by revisionists that the America of the past becomes truly dead and gone. The foundations of this nation were thought out so deeply, laid so carefully, and poured so completely that they can indeed endure a very diverse people, an array of problems, and many other assorted things. But what it cannot survive is division and neglect. *E pluribus unum*, "out of many one," requires that in spite of our differences we still look out for each other.

It's not easy to put yourself aside and be willing to work in agreement with someone who may not live the way you live and do everything the way you do, but if we are to continue on, it will be required. Living divided is easy; working together is indeed hard. Seclusion and separation are fueled by passion and pride, unity and commonality of cause are the by-product of humility and self-determination. Individual ideals are loud and obnoxious things; the willingness to build bridges is the work of the Lord. That is why I believe, more now than ever, that the Founding Fathers felt it appropriate to say, "In God we trust." The *we* truly says it all.

Step 5.5: A House Divided

- There is a race to see who is willing to work together to accomplish their common agenda in this nation.

- When you make the major things minor and the minor things major, you isolate yourself every time.

- Faith should be a unifying factor, not a divisive one.

Questions to Consider

1. Am I doing my part to walk in agreement with others who are not exactly like me, or do I allow walls of separation to keep me divided from them?

   _____

   _____

2. Am I willing to get over the little things so that I can join with others to accomplish the big things?

   _____

   _____

Step 5.6

THE GOOD FIGHT IS STILL WORTH FIGHTING FOR

THERE IS A very close correlation between the words etched in the marble of the Jefferson Memorial and those written by the apostle Paul to his pupil Timothy. Paul said, "Fight the good fight of faith" (1 Timothy 6:12). Jefferson, in his own words, is memorialized with: "I have sworn upon the altar of God, eternal hostility against every form of tyranny over the mind of man."[1] Both battles were fought on a personal level to see that others had the opportunity to live free. Jefferson saw the battlefield of tyranny as the mind. The Bible also tells us we wage our spiritual war between our ears: "Casting down arguments and every high thing that exalts itself against the knowledge of God" (2 Corinthians 10:5). Knowledge is as much a mental matter as the tyranny of the mind to which Jefferson referred.

From his own words we can see that Jefferson felt his cause to be a holy one. Otherwise it would not have been a vow on the "altar of God." We can also see he did not apply it to the nation as a whole but to the individual. The message is a powerful one. How do you change a nation? One person at a time. This is why it is imperative to understand the four battlefields that the good fight of faith and freedom are to be fought on.

Your Personal Fight

The first battlefield begins where Jefferson left off: your personal fight. You may limit this to your individual vote, or you may extend it to an organization you work with or for in an effort to overcome an evil that you have determined must be erased. But the fact remains that if you are unwilling to do anything on a personal level, you cannot expect much to be done on any other level.

Knowledge has always been power, and personal knowledge brings personal power. One of the tactics that unrighteous rulers often use is to twist, distort, and spin the truth. Washington is not immune to this practice, but that doesn't mean that you have to fall prey to it. One of the best ways to win your personal battle is to stay informed. Do not be apathetic in the area of intelligence; ingest what you can about what each candidate is doing and why, and then, when the time comes, use your vote as a voice of affirmation for those who are doing a good job and a shout of protest for those who need to be replaced.

Within Your Home

The second battlefield for freedom from individual tyranny is within the walls of your home. I am not suggesting you sign your children up for the Young Republicans and have them wear campaign buttons to school, but I am telling you that you are responsible to make your children aware of the environment and the world that they are living in. It is only through teaching your children about the days in which they live that they will have an idea about what needs to be done and what role they should play.

If you saw a stranger in the park, I am certain you would unashamedly inform your child about the threat and risk of trusting him. You would go through all the possible scenarios that could endanger him or her: "Don't take candy from him; it may be poison." "Don't get in the car with him; he may harm you." "Don't talk to him or go near him; he cannot be trusted." Why should you approach politics any differently? Why not tell your children who is doing a good job and who is not, and why they are not, and what a good job looks like so they have a clue what to look for. Some may think, "Well, I don't want to impress my opinion on them." You are their parent; that is what you are supposed to do.

Within the Church

The third arena in the good fight of individual faith and freedom is the church. This should be the base camp for the cause, because the church is the one place where you get to apply God's truth to all areas of life. The Bible is the standard for everything, including the government, and it should be so today. In order for it to happen, the church needs to be full of individuals who are willing to engage in the fight against what Jefferson called "tyranny over the mind of man." The church has to do a lot more than just entertain its members for a few hours on Sunday and make them glad they came to service. We must equip every person who walks through the doors so they can be successful in the ongoing war between truth and deception, light and darkness.

The Bible says, "My people are destroyed for lack of knowledge" (Hosea 4:6). The leaders of the church are held accountable for the knowledge they impart or refuse to impart to their congregation. I have heard some preachers piously tell me, "I don't think that topic has a place in the house of God." Their piety is a camouflage for cowardice, because every topic has a place in the house of God. With the right amount of determination and study, every minister should be ready and willing to talk about it. Second Timothy 2:15 states: "Be diligent to present yourself approved to God, a worker who does not need to be ashamed, rightly dividing the word of truth." The Bible has something to say about everything, and therefore we shouldn't be afraid to approach anything.

Within the Government

Finally, the biggest and most difficult battlefield of them all is the government itself. Our government desperately needs a blood transfusion of truth and righteousness. Why? Because society can never rise above its leaders. Pathetic leaders; pathetic land. Great leaders; great land.

Skim through your history book and see if I am not right. I referred earlier to Paul encouraging us to tear down "every high thing that exalts itself against the knowledge of God" (2 Corinthians 10:5). There is none higher in the realm of government than the mythological wall between the church and state.

sYes, they are distinct institutions with areas of jurisdiction, oversight, and responsibility, but they were not intended to work apart from each other; they were intended to work together. To say that the church has no say-so in how society is governed is lunacy, because all law has religious foundations. Who is it that sits and watches over the threshold of the Supreme Court where decisions are made on ongoing basis that routinely defy God? It is none other than Moses, the original lawgiver, who received what he etched in stone from Jehovah God Himself.

This reality is something Jefferson and those who walked with him recognized. This is why they ratified a document that declared every man was "endowed by their Creator with certain unalienable Rights."[2] This phrase is not placed there because they felt it was poetic—it's there because they believed it, and we should too. The church's job is to make sure the state and its citizens do not lose sight of the truth, and the state's job is to make sure the church is free to continue.

When everyone begins to play the role they are responsible for, then and only then will the tide in the good fight of faith begin to turn, and the freedom that God endowed us with will become a reality in the nation we all love. We have a role to play, and we cannot leave it up to the next Thomas Jefferson. We must each do what we can to ensure that our country is blessed, our heritage in honored, and our children's futures are secure. The best way I know to do this is see to it that we fulfill Psalm 33:12: "Blessed is the nation whose God is the LORD."

Step 5.6: The Good Fight Is Still Worth Fighting For

- Everyone has a role in the fight of faith and freedom.

- Knowledge is power, and personal knowledge is personal power.

- Psalm 33:12: "Blessed is the nation whose God is the Lord."

Questions to Consider

1. Am I doing my part to ensure that others have the opportunity to live in freedom from tyranny over the minds of men?

   _____

   _____

2. Where can I improve my effort and involvement to see that the good fight of faith and freedom is won?

   _____

   _____

Step 5.7

THERE IS NO SUCH THING AS ABSOLUTE FREEDOM

REMEMBER THAT IN the introduction of this section I told you that the topic of faith and freedom was a complex thing? Well, allow me to add to the complexity with this final thought: *there is no such thing as absolute freedom.* Everything lives under the authority and governance of something or someone else. Consider this in nature; nothing is absolutely free. Birds may be free to fly, but should they try to soar out of our atmosphere, they would find themselves hindered from doing so. Fish are free to swim the ocean, but they are not free to leave it, because doing so would destroy them. The solar system is not free. The sun has a course, as do the planets and every moon, and star. The oceans are not free; they have defined borders that they may try to invade from time to time, but eventually they are pushed back and confined. And you and I are not absolutely free.

We have the absolute freedom to choose the life that we see as best, but the moment the choice is made, we are set in its course and ways. The life we have to choose in large scale is a choice between the two worldviews: the God-centered one or the man-centered one. When you choose between those two, you have locked yourself into the limitations and extents that come with the decision. You are no longer absolutely free.

Should you choose the God-centered worldview, you are free to enjoy all that it affords. Peace instead of turmoil, joy instead of sorrow, hope instead of despair, confidence rather than insecurity—all of these by-products are only a portion of the life of faith that you are free to choose but confined to live. When you choose a life of faith, you are not free to violate God's law; no one is, not even the godless. In spite of their every effort to scoff at it, God's law breaks even those who choose against it; they cannot break it.

That's the large-scale choice you have to make, but throughout this book, in section after section, page after page, you have seen the personal decisions you have to make also, which reiterate this resounding truth: there is no such thing as absolute freedom. If you are going to see the personal turnaround that you are looking for, you will need to be subject to the personal revolution in which you are going to engage. You are not free to do whatever you want, whenever you want, and expect the change. Your change comes by a life of discipline, which is not absolute freedom.

If you are married, you are not absolutely free. You had the freedom to make a choice, and the day you said, "I do," you were confined to the choice that you made. Granted, you confined yourself to a lifetime commitment of honoring, cherishing, loving, and supporting one another. You confined yourself to the life that God truly designed you to crave and enjoy, but you are confined nonetheless and are not absolutely free.

As a parent, I am not absolutely free. I am held to the responsibility to provide for, protect, influence, educate, and unconditionally love my children. There isn't a decision I make where their existence doesn't impact me. "How will this affect my children?" "Is it in their best interest as much as it is mine?" "Will I as a father regret having to explain my behavior to one of my sons?" All of these questions confine my behavior in a manner that clearly demonstrates I am not free.

Consider your citizenship. You live in the *land of the free*, but you are held by its laws. If you want to test this statement, refuse to pay your taxes, or drive seventy-five miles an hour in a twenty-mile-per-hour school zone. You will learn a great deal about the limitations of your freedom. No matter how you examine it, we keep coming back to this fact: there is no such thing as absolute freedom.

The best part of coming to this reality is that you find the quality of your confinement determines the quality of your life. If you choose to confine yourself to the role of being the best parent you can be, by God's grace, you will enjoy the most glorious treasure that you would ever hope to find—children who are a source of honor to their mother and father and a force for good and not evil. That, my friend, is a high-quality life. Consider your spouse. The quality of your choice determines the quality of your life, but before you get carried away and start picking on your partner, keep in mind that person is the one who confined himself or herself to you.

When you choose a nation to live in, your nation determines the quality of your life, and I believe that there is still no greater choice than the United States of America. I laugh when I hear people comment that if this or that happens they are going to leave the country. In some cases I truly wish they would make good on the promise, but the truth is, where are you going to go and find another place like this one? We may have our areas that truly need a genuine change, but the glorious news is that in this nation we are free to change it! We do not have to ask permission to defend our ideals; they are ours, and no one can take them away. You are not free in this nation to write your own Declaration of Independence and plant your own flag in your front yard and create the United State of Your Own Self, but thankfully, because of that document, you are free to pursue happiness as you so choose.

That choice includes the freedom of faith in God. Remember, the quality of your confinement determines the quality of your life. When you are confined as a servant of the living God, and He counts you as one of His own, the life you are confined to live will be beyond all you could ask, think, or imagine.

There are a lot of choices to be made. Some lead to dictatorships and others to a life of liberty. The choices you make will either revolutionize your life or create the need for a major turnaround. No matter which one it is, remember you are responsible to determine how the road is paved. Do not take the task lightly or consider it a small matter. If you walk in the right direction one step at a time, you can truly make a difference and change the world. Refuse to live and die beneath your destiny, and understand you have the power to create the turnaround that you need.

Section 5 Review: Seven Lessons to Make a Political Difference

5.1. Consider a new kind of party.

5.2. Self-government is the highest form of government.

5.3. You are what He is looking for.

5.4. Recognize the political action of the kingdom.

5.5. A house divided will not stand.

5.6. The good fight is still worth fighting for.

5.7. There's no such thing as absolute freedom.

Question to Consider

1. What are you waiting for? Get started!

_____

_____

_____

Epilogue

A S MY FATHER'S son I am often asked, "So what's it like being John Hagee's boy?" I hope you've learned from this manuscript that I wouldn't trade it for the world. It has made me who I am and has afforded me opportunities more than I could dream of. At times people will take issue with some of my perspectives, and I have the distinct pleasure of telling them, "It's the way I was raised."

Whether you choose to or choose not to implement in your own life any of what you have read in this book, at least when you put it down you will know what makes me, *me* and why I do what *I* do. It is because I have a father who has demonstrated the courage to take on the world when he felt the cause was just. He has sacrificed selflessly when he knew the need was great. He lived by principle because he knew we were watching and loved us unconditionally in ways no words can describe. He has taught me how to be *response-able* and to believe I can make a difference every day on some level in someone's life.

I pray that by my sharing with you just a few things he has taught me, you'll begin to believe you can make a difference and become *response-able* too.

Notes

Foreword

1. The Churchill Centre and Museum, "The Price of Greatness Is Responsibility," http://www.winstonchurchill.org/component/content/article/3-speeches/420-the-price-of-greatness-is-responsibility (accessed February 11, 2011).

Step 1.6—You May Lose a Battle, but Don't Lose the War

1. The Churchill Centre and Museum, "London Opera House, 11 September 1914," http://www.winstonchurchill.org/component/content/article/16-quotes/424-london-opera-house-11-september-1914 (accessed February 11, 2011).

Section 4—Educational Response-Ability

1. Barna Group, "Americans Are Most Likely to Base Truth on Feelings," Barna Update, February 12, 2002, http://www.barna.org/barna-update/article/5-barna-update/67-americans-are-most-likely-to-base-truth-on-feelings (accessed February 16, 2011).

Step 4.1—Stop Outsourcing Your Authority

1. Becky Barrow, "19 Minutes—How Long Working Parents Give Their Children," *Daily Mail*, July 19, 2006, http://www.dailymail.co.uk/news/article-396609/19-minutes--long-working-parents-children.html (accessed February 5, 2011).

2. Michael O'Brien, "53 Republicans Demand Firing of 'Safe Schools Czar' Kevin Jennings," *The Hill's Blog Briefing Room* (blog), October 15, 2009, http://thehill.com/blogs/blog-briefing-room/news/63249-53-republicans-demand-firing-of-safe-schools-czar (accessed February 5, 2011).

3. Maxim Loft, "Obama's 'Safe Schools' Czar Admits He Poorly Handled Underage Sex Case," FOXNews.com, September 30, 2009, http://www.foxnews.com/politics/2009/09/30/obamas-safe-schools-czar-admits-poorly-handled-underage-sex-case/ (accessed February 5, 2010).

4. Ibid.

Step 4.4—Get Them While They Are Young

1. *Victorian Thoroughbred Newsletter*, "Quote of the Week," Racing Australia (blog), January 16, 2011, http://racingwithvin.blogspot.com/ (accessed

February 16, 2011). This quote can also be found on various quotation sites online.

Section 5—Political Response-Ability

1. Alex Barnett, ed., *Words That Changed America* (Guilford, CT: The Lyon's Press, 2003).
2. Frank Moore, ed., *The Patriot Preachers of the American Revolution* (New York: n.p., 1860), 105.

Step 5.4—The Political Action of the Kingdom

1. "Let Our Hearts Be Stout," a prayer by the president of the United States, *New York Times*, June 7, 1944. Also, Franklin D. Roosevelt Presidential Library and Museum, "D-Day Prayer," June 6, 1944, http://docs.fdrlibrary.marist.edu/ DDAYPR32.HTML (accessed February 16, 2011).

Step 5.5—A House Divided

1. John Adams, letter to Abigail Adams, April 15, 1776, available at the Massachusetts Historical Society, http://www.masshist.org/digitaladams/aea/ cfm/doc.cfm?id=L17760415ja (accessed February 18, 2011); also quoted in James H. Hutson, *The Founders on Religion* (Princeton, NJ: Princeton University Press, 2007), 48.
2. George Washington, address to Irish immigrants, draft handwritten by David Humphries, December 2, 1783, The Charters of Freedom, National Archives and Records Administration, http://www.archives.gov/exhibits/ charters/charters_of_freedom_12.html (accessed February 18, 2011).
3. George Washington, letter to Tench Tilghman, March 24, 1784, quoted in Paul F. Boller, *George Washington and Religion* (Dallas: Southern Methodist University Press, 1963), 118.

Step 5.6—The Good Fight Is Still Worth Fighting For

1. Thomas Jefferson, letter to Benjamin Rush, September 23, 1800, transcript viewed at "The Thomas Jefferson Papers," Library of Congress, http://memory .loc.gov/cgi-bin/query/r?ammem/mtj:@field(DOCID+@lit(tj090069)) (accessed February 18, 2011).
2. Charters of Freedom, "The Declaration of Independence," National Archives and Records Administration, http://www.archives.gov/exhibits/ charters/declaration_transcript.html (accessed February 18, 2011).